Forever I Will Sing

Responsorial Psalm Chants
& Gospel Acclamations

December 2, 2018 – November 28, 2019

Year C

Music by Timothy R. Smith

Online Instructional Videos

Visit www.timothyrsmith.com for links to online instructional videos for each of the Responsorial Psalms and Gospel Acclamations. These are helpful in familiarizing cantors and instrumentalists with each piece.

Refrain Melodies for Assembly Worship Aids

To receive pdf of all refrain melodies at no additional charge, send copy of receipt to **forever@timothyrsmith.com**

Forever I Will Sing

Responsorial Psalm Chants and Gospel Acclamations
Year C – December 2, 2018 through November 28, 2019

Musical settings by Timothy R. Smith
This songbook © 2018, Timothy R. Smith. Published by TR TUNE, LLC. All rights reserved.
www.timothyrsmith.com
ISBN 978-0996812832
(TR TUNE, LLC)

Publisher:	TR TUNE, LLC, Waterford, MI www.timothyrsmith.com
Composer:	Timothy R. Smith
Editor:	Barbara Bridge
Cover Art:	Mary Dudek
	www.marydudekart.com

Special Thanks…
Rick Modlin and all the people at OCP; to Barbara Bridge, for her encouragement and tireless eye to detail; to Mary Dudek for her great artwork, to Father Scott Thibodeau, Father Brian Meldrum, the parish and music ministry of Our Lady of the Lakes, for their support and openness to singing these settings. Thank you to my family: Emily, Gabe, Al and my dear wife Kim, who shows so much patience for her husband and his laptop appendage. This book is dedicated to the memory of my Mom and Dad, Mary Clare Smith and Gary Smith. To God be the glory!

We are still developing and refining this format and we welcome any feedback. Please feel free to contact me anytime if you have feedback about any aspect of this publication.
Tim Smith
tim@timothyrsmith.com

Singing the Psalm Settings

Psalm Refrains can be adapted to piano, organ, guitar accompaniment, or even SATB choir. The melodies, rhythms and harmonies are designed to embody the spirit of the text.

Verse Chants are set for solo voice (Cantor) with sustained keyboard or guitar accompaniment.

General Directives for Chanting the Verses

Consider the example below for a discussion of the various musical elements:

In the chanted verses, the music follows the "speech rhythm" of the text, flowing smoothly so that the text is understood and its meaning is clear.

Black notes indicate that all the verses have only one syllable on that note.

Open notes indicate that at least one verse has multiple syllables on the open note. Where there is only one syllable on an open note, the cantor should sing that syllable as though it is a black note–not sustaining that syllable–but maintaining the speech rhythm of the text.

The Right Slash " / " indicates that one phrase ends and a new phrase begins on the same note, with a slight pause at the end of the phrase before the slash. For example, at the end of Verse 2a there is a pause between "creatures;" and "bless" to distinguish between the two phrases.

Braces "{ }" act as repeat signs. For example, at the end of Verse 4a, the right bracket "}" indicates a repeat to the left bracket "{" at 4b. Thus, the cantor connects 4a and 4b to complete the phrase, "they are created, and you renew the face of the earth." The braces in Verse 2a, 2b, and 2c, direct the cantor to connect all three lines: "the earth is full of your creatures; bless the Lord, O my soul! Alleluia!"

Square Brackets "[ ]" indicate a repetition of words or phrases from the original text.

Page	Sunday	Refrain	Psalm Reference
90	Second Sunday of Easter (or Sunday of Divine Mercy)	Give thanks to the Lord	Psalm 118:2-4, 13-15, 22-24
92	Third Sunday of Easter	I will praise you, Lord	Psalm 30:2, 4, 5-6, 11-12, 13
94	Fourth Sunday of Easter	We are his people	Psalm 100:1-2, 3, 5
96	Fifth Sunday of Easter	I will praise your name forever	Psalm 145:8-9, 10-11, 12-13
98	Sixth Sunday of Easter	O God, let all the nations	Psalm 67:2-3, 5, 6, 8
100	The Ascension of the Lord	God mounts his throne	Psalm 47:2-3, 6-7, 8-9
102	Seventh Sunday of Easter	The Lord is king	Psalm 97:1-2, 6-7, 9
104	Pentecost Sunday: Extended Vigil Mass	Blessed the people the Lord has chosen	Psalm 33:10-11, 12-13, 14-15
106	Pentecost Sunday: Extended Vigil Mass	Glory and praise forever	Daniel 3:52, 53, 54, 55, 56
108	Pentecost Sunday: Extended Vigil Mass	Lord, you have the words	Psalm 19:8, 9, 10, 11
110	Pentecost Sunday: Extended Vigil Mass	Give thanks to the Lord	Psalm 107:2-3, 4-5, 6-7, 8-9
112	Pentecost Sunday: Extended Vigil Mass	Lord, send out your Spirit	Psalm 104:1-2, 24 & 35, 27-28, 29-30
114	Pentecost Sunday: At the Mass during the Day	Lord, send out your Spirit	Psalm 104:1, 24, 29-30, 31, 34
116	The Most Holy Trinity	O Lord, our God,	Psalm 8:4-5, 6-7, 8-9
118	The Most Holy Body and Blood of Christ	You are a priest forever	Psalm 110:1, 2, 3, 4
120	13th Sunday in Ordinary Time	You are my inheritance	Psalm 16:1-2, 5, 7-8, 9-10, 11
122	14th Sunday in Ordinary Time	Let all the earth cry out to God	Psalm 66:1-3, 4-5, 6-7, 16, 20
124	15th Sunday in Ordinary Time	Turn to the Lord in your need	Psalm 69:14, 17, 30-31, 33-34, 36, 37
126	16th Sunday in Ordinary Time	He who does justice	Psalm 15:2-3, 3-4, 5
128	17th Sunday in Ordinary Time	Lord, on the day I called	Psalm 138:1-2, 2-3, 6-7, 7-8
130	18th Sunday in Ordinary Time	If today you hear his voice	Psalm 90:3-4, 5-6, 12-13, 14, 17
132	19th Sunday in Ordinary Time	Blessed the people	Psalm 33:1, 12, 18-19, 20-22
134	The Assumption of the Blessed Virgin Mary: Vigil Mass	Lord, go up to your place of rest	Psalm 132:6-7, 9-10, 13-14
136	The Assumption of the Blessed Virgin Mary: During the Day	The queen stands at your right hand	Psalm 45:10, 11, 12, 16
138	20th Sunday in Ordinary Time	Lord, come to my aid	Psalm 40:2, 3, 4, 18
140	21st Sunday in Ordinary Time	Go out to all the world	Psalm 117:1, 2
142	22nd Sunday in Ordinary Time	God, in your goodness	Psalm 68:4-5, 6-7, 10-11
144	23rd Sunday in Ordinary Time	In every age	Psalm 90:3-4, 5-6, 12-13, 14, 17
146	24th Sunday in Ordinary Time	I will rise and go to my father	Psalm 51:3-4, 12-13, 17, 19
148	25th Sunday in Ordinary Time	Praise the Lord who lifts up the poor	Psalm 113:1-2, 4-6, 7-8
150	26th Sunday in Ordinary Time	Praise the Lord, my soul	Psalm 146:7, 8-9, 9-10
152	27th Sunday in Ordinary Time	If today you hear his voice	Psalm 95:1-2, 6-7, 8-9
154	28th Sunday in Ordinary Time	The Lord has revealed to the nations	Psalm 98:1, 2-3, 3-4
156	29th Sunday in Ordinary Time	Our help is from the Lord	Psalm 121:1-2, 3-4, 5-6, 7-8
158	30th Sunday in Ordinary Time	The Lord hears the cry of the poor	Psalm 34:2-3, 17-18, 19, 23
160	All Saints	Lord, this is the people	Psalm 24:1bc-2, 3-4ab, 5-6
162	31st Sunday in Ordinary Time	I will praise your name forever	Psalm 145:1-2, 8-9, 10-11, 13, 14
164	32nd Sunday in Ordinary Time	Lord, when your glory appears	Psalm 17:1, 5-6, 8, 15
166	33rd Sunday in Ordinary Time	The Lord comes to rule the earth	Psalm 98:5-6, 7-8, 9
168	Our Lord Jesus Christ, King of the Universe	Let us go rejoicing	Psalm 122:1-2, 3-4, 4-5
170	Thanksgiving Day	Blessed be the name of the Lord	Psalm 113:1-2, 3-4, 5-6, 7-8
172	Rite of Entrance into the Order of Catechumens	Blessed the people	Psalm 33:4-5, 12-13, 18-19, 20 & 22
174	Selected Psalm for Weddings	Blessed are those who fear the Lord	Psalm 128:1-2, 3, 4-5
175	Selected Psalm for Funerals	The Lord is kind and merciful	Psalm 103:8 & 10, 13-14, 15-16, 17-18
176	Selected Common (Seasonal) Psalm for Ordinary Time	The Lord is my light and my salvation	Psalm 27:1, 4, 13-14

Responsorial Psalm Index

Page	SCRIPTURE REFERENCE
106	Daniel 3:52, 53, 54, 55, 56
78	Exodus 15:1-2, 3-4, 5-6, 17-18
16	Isaiah 12:2-3, 4, 5-6
81	Isaiah 12:2-3, 4, 5-6
84	Isaiah 12:2-3, 4bcd, 5-6
14	Judith 13:18bcde, 19
44	Psalm1:1-2, 3, 4 & 6
116	Psalm 8:4-5, 6-7, 8-9
126	Psalm 15:2-3, 3-4, 5
120	Psalm 16:1-2, 5, 7-8, 9-10, 11
76	Psalm 16:5, 8, 9-10, 11
164	Psalm 17:1, 5-6, 8, 15
82	Psalm 19:8, 9, 10, 11
38	Psalm 19:8, 9, 10, 15
108	Psalm 19:8, 9, 10, 11
68	Psalm 22:8-9, 17-18, 19-20, 23-24
62	Psalm 23:1-3a, 3b-4, 5, 6
160	Psalm 24:1bc-2, 3-4ab, 5-6
8	Psalm 25:4-5, 8-9, 10, 14
176	Psalm 27:1, 4, 13-14
54	Psalm 27:1, 7-8, 8-9, 13-14
80	Psalm 30:2, 4, 5-6, 11-12, 13
92	Psalm 30:2, 4, 5-6, 11-12, 13
72	Psalm 31:2, 6, 12-13, 15-16, 17, 25
132	Psalm 33:1, 12, 18-19, 20-22
104	Psalm 33:10-11, 12-13, 14-15
172	Psalm 33:4-5, 12-13, 18-19, 20 & 22
75	Psalm 33:4-5, 6-7, 12-13, 20 & 22
158	Psalm 34:2-3, 17-18, 19, 23
60	Psalm 34:2-3, 4-5, 6-7
138	Psalm 40:2, 3, 4, 18
83	Psalm 42:3, 5; 43:3, 4
136	Psalm 45:10, 11, 12, 16
100	Psalm 47:2-3, 6-7, 8-9
85	Psalm 51:12-13, 14-15, 18-19
146	Psalm 51:3-4, 12-13, 17, 19
50	Psalm 51:3-4, 5-6ab, 12-13, 14 & 17
122	Psalm 66:1-3, 4-5, 6-7, 16, 20
30	Psalm 67:2-3, 5, 6, 8
98	Psalm 67:2-3, 5, 6, 8
142	Psalm 68:4-5, 6-7, 10-11
124	Psalm 69:14, 17, 30-31, 33-34, 36, 37
40	Psalm 71:1-2, 3-4, 5-6, 15, 17
32	Psalm 72:1-2, 7-8, 10-11, 12-13
18	Psalm 80:2-3, 15-16, 18-19

Page	SCRIPTURE REFERENCE
28	Psalm 84:2-3, 5-6, 9-10
20	Psalm 89:4-5, 16-17, 27, 29
144	Psalm 90:3-4, 5-6, 12-13, 14, 17
130	Psalm 90:3-4, 5-6, 12-13, 14 & 17
52	Psalm 91:1-2, 10-11, 12-13, 14-15
48	Psalm 92:2-3, 13-14, 15-16
58	Psalm 95:1-2, 6-7, 8-9
152	Psalm 95:1-2, 6-7, 8-9
22	Psalm 96:1-2, 2-3, 11-12, 13
36	Psalm 96:1-2, 2-3, 7-8, 9-10
102	Psalm 97:1-2, 6-7, 9
24	Psalm 97:1, 6, 11-12
154	Psalm 98:1, 2-3, 3-4
26	Psalm 98:1, 2-3, 3-4, 5-6
10	Psalm 98:1, 2-3ab, 3cd-4
166	Psalm 98:5-6, 7-8, 9
94	Psalm 100:1-2, 3, 5
56	Psalm 103:1-2, 3-4, 6-7, 8, 11
46	Psalm 103:1-2, 3-4, 8, 10, 12-13
175	Psalm 103:8 & 10, 13-14, 15-16, 17-18
112	Psalm 104:1-2, 24 & 35, 27-28, 29-30
74	Psalm 104:1-2, 5-6, 10, 12, 13-14, 24, 35
114	Psalm 104:1, 24, 29-30, 31, 34
34	Psalm 104:1b-2, 3-4, 24-25, 27-28, 29-30
110	Psalm 107:2-3, 4-5, 6-7, 8-9
118	Psalm 110:1, 2, 3, 4
170	Psalm 113:1-2, 3-4, 5-6, 7-8
148	Psalm 113:1-2, 4-6, 7-8
70	Psalm 116:12-13, 15-16bc, 17-18
140	Psalm 117:1, 2
86	Psalm 118:1-2, 16-17, 22-23
88	Psalm 118:1-2, 16-17, 22-23
90	Psalm 118:2-4, 13-15, 22-24
156	Psalm 121:1-2, 3-4, 5-6, 7-8
168	Psalm 122:1-2, 3-4, 4-5
12	Psalm 126:1-2, 2-3, 4-5, 6
64	Psalm 126:1-2, 2-3, 4-5, 6
174	Psalm 128:1-2, 3, 4-5
66	Psalm 130:1-2, 3-4, 5-6, 7-8
134	Psalm 132:6-7, 9-10, 13-14
42	Psalm 138:1-2, 2-3, 4-5, 7-8
128	Psalm 138:1-2, 2-3, 6-7, 7-8
162	Psalm 145:1-2, 8-9, 10-11, 13, 14
96	Psalm 145:8-9, 10-11, 12-13
150	Psalm 146:7, 8-9, 9-10

Responsorial Psalm Refrain Alphabetical Index

Page	REFRAIN
24	A light will shine on us this day
26	All the ends of the earth
86	Alleluia (Easter Vigil Gospel Acclamation)
50	Be merciful, O Lord
52	Be with me, Lord
28	Blessed are they who dwell
44	Blessed are they who hope in the Lord.
174	Blessed are those who fear the Lord
170	Blessed be the name of the Lord
132	Blessed the people the Lord has chosen
172	Blessed the people the Lord has chosen
104	Blessed the people the Lord has chosen
85	Create a clean heart
16	Cry out with joy and gladness
72	Father, into your hands I commend
20	Forever I will sing
90	Give thanks to the Lord (Psalm 118)
110	Give thanks to the Lord (Psalm 107)
106	Glory and praise forever!
140	Go out to all the world
100	God mounts his throne
142	God, in your goodness
126	He who does justice
80	I will praise you, Lord
92	I will praise you, Lord
96	I will praise your name forever
162	I will praise your name forever
146	I will rise and go to my father
40	I will sing of your salvation
58	If today you hear his voice
130	If today you hear his voice
152	If today you hear his voice
144	In every age
42	In the sight of the angels
122	Let all the earth cry out to God
168	Let us go rejoicing
78	Let us sing to the Lord
83	Like a deer
48	Lord it is good to give thanks to you.
138	Lord, come to my aid
32	Lord, every nation on earth
134	Lord, go up to your place of your rest
18	Lord, make us turn to you
128	Lord, on the day I called
74	Lord, send out your Spirit

Page	REFRAIN
112	Lord, send out your Spirit
114	Lord, send out your Spirit
160	Lord, this is the people
164	Lord, when your glory appears
82	Lord, you have the words
108	Lord, you have the words
30	May God bless us in his mercy
68	My God, my God,
34	O bless the Lord, my soul
98	O God, let all the nations
116	O Lord, our God,
70	Our blessing cup
156	Our help is from the Lord
148	Praise the Lord who lifts up the poor
150	Praise the Lord, my soul
36	Proclaim his marvelous deeds
10	Sing to the Lord a new song
60	Taste and see
75	The earth is full
166	The Lord comes to rule the earth
12	The Lord has done great things
64	The Lord has done great things
154	The Lord has revealed to the nations
158	The Lord hears the cry of the poor
56	The Lord is kind and merciful
175	The Lord is kind and merciful
46	The Lord is kind and merciful.
102	The Lord is king
54	The Lord is my light and my salvation
176	The Lord is my light and my salvation
62	The Lord is my shepherd
136	The queen stands at your right hand
88	This is the day
8	To you, O Lord, I Lift My Soul
22	Today is born our savior
124	Turn to the Lord in your need
94	We are his people
66	With the Lord there is mercy
118	You are a priest forever
76	You are my inheritance
120	You are my inheritance
14	You are the highest honor
81	You will draw water
84	You will draw water
38	Your words, Lord, are Spirit and life

7

First Sunday of Advent

December 2

Psalm 25:4-5, 8-9, 10, 14

Gospel Acclamation: Psalm 85:8

Acclamation: (Keyboard/SATB) NO. III

(M.M. ♩ = c. 160)

Verse: (Cantor)

Show us, Lord, your love; / and grant us your sal - vation.

The Immaculate Conception of the Blessed Virgin Mary

December 8

Psalm 98:1, 2-3ab, 3cd-4

Gospel Acclamation: Luke 1:28

Acclamation: (Keyboard/SATB) NO. IV

Verse: (Cantor)

Second Sunday of Advent

December 9

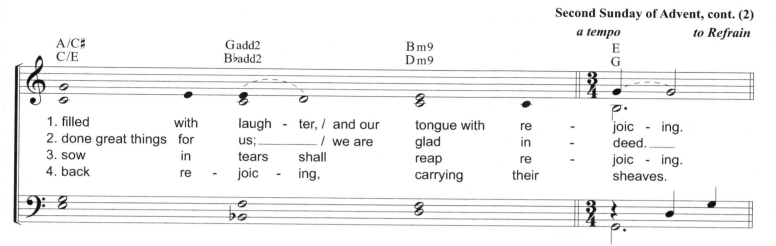

Gospel Acclamation: Luke 3:4, 6

Acclamation: (Keyboard/SATB) NO. I

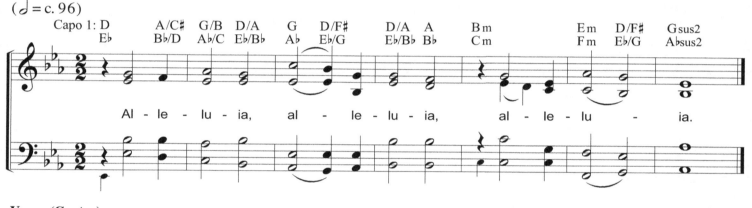

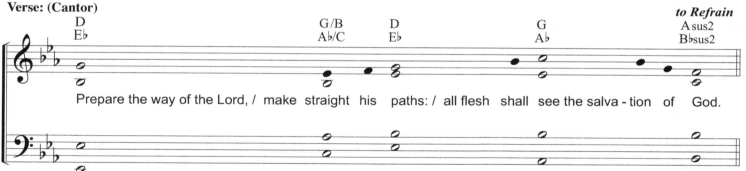

Our Lady of Guadalupe

December 12

Judith 13:18bcde, 19

* *Added line*

Gospel Acclamation: cf. Psalm 85:8

Acclamation: (Keyboard/SATB) NO. II

(M.M. ♩ = c. 130)

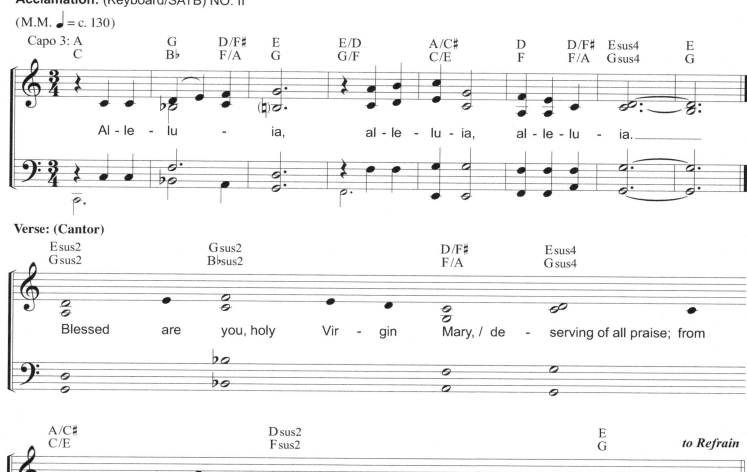

Al - le - lu - ia, al - le - lu - ia, al - le - lu - ia.

Verse: (Cantor)

Blessed are you, holy Vir - gin Mary, / de - serving of all praise; from

you rose the sun of justice, Christ our God.

to Refrain

Third Sunday of Advent

December 16

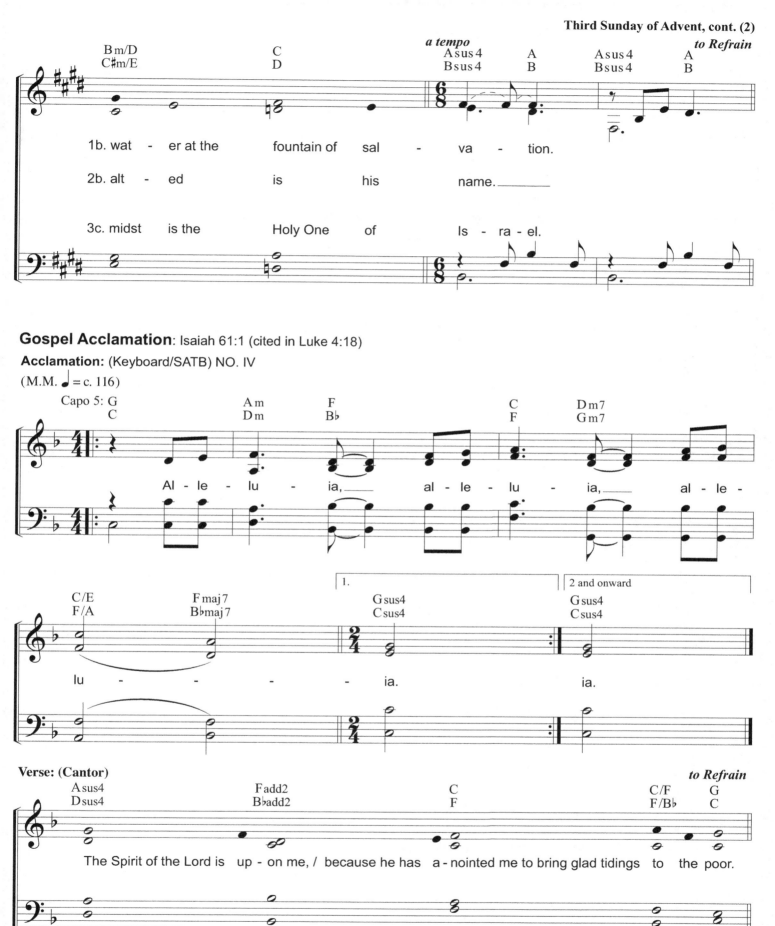

Gospel Acclamation: Isaiah 61:1 (cited in Luke 4:18)

Acclamation: (Keyboard/SATB) NO. IV

(M.M. ♩ = c. 116)

Al - le - lu - ia, ___ al - le - lu - ia, ___ al - le -

lu - - - - ia. ia.

Verse: (Cantor) *to Refrain*

The Spirit of the Lord is up - on me, / because he has a - nointed me to bring glad tidings to the poor.

Fourth Sunday of Advent

December 23

Psalm 80:2-3, 15-16, 18-19

Gospel Acclamation: Luke 1:38

Acclamation: (Keyboard/SATB) NO. II

(M.M. ♩ = c. 130)

Al - le - lu - ia, al - le - lu - ia, al - le - lu - ia._____

Verse: (Cantor)

to Refrain

Behold, I am the handmaid of the Lord. / May it be done to me ac - cord - ing to your word.

The Nativity of The Lord (Christmas): At the Vigil Mass

December 24

Gospel Acclamation:

Acclamation: (Keyboard/SATB) NO. V

(M.M. ♪ = c. 150)

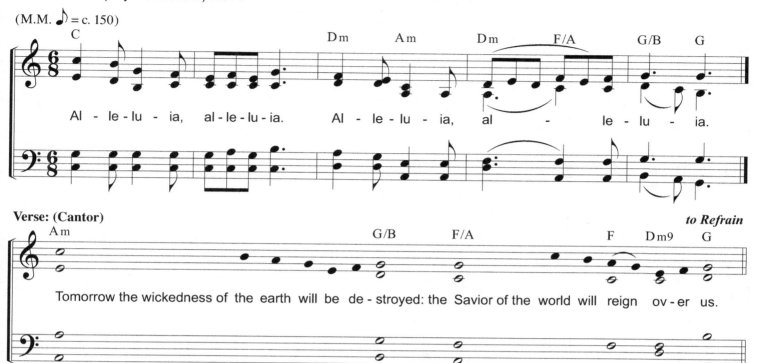

Al - le -lu - ia, al -le -lu - ia. Al - le -lu - ia, al - le - lu - ia.

Verse: (Cantor)

to Refrain

Tomorrow the wickedness of the earth will be de - stroyed: the Savior of the world will reign ov-er us.

The Nativity of the Lord (Christmas): At the Mass during the Night

December 25

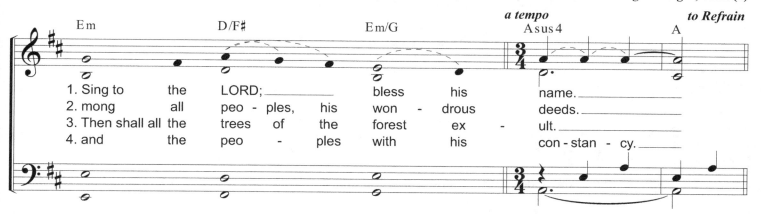

1. Sing to the LORD;_____ bless his name._____
2. mong all peo - ples, his won - drous deeds._____
3. Then shall all the trees of the forest ex - ult._____
4. and the peo - ples with his con - stan - cy._____

Gospel Acclamation: Luke 2:10-11

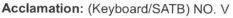

Acclamation: (Keyboard/SATB) NO. V

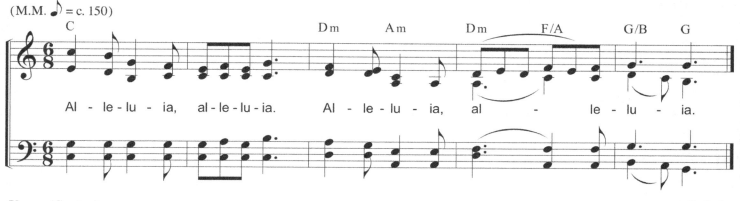

Al - le - lu - ia, al - le - lu - ia. Al - le - lu - ia, al - le - lu - ia.

Verse: (Cantor) *to Refrain*

I proclaim to you good news of great joy: / to - day a Sav - ior is born for us, Christ the Lord.

The Nativity of the Lord (Christmas): At the Mass at Dawn

December 25

Psalm 97:1, 6, 11-12

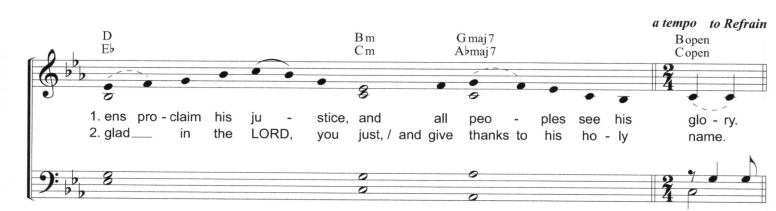

Gospel Acclamation: Luke 2:14

Acclamation: (Keyboard/SATB) NO. V

(M.M. ♪ = c. 150)

Al - le - lu - ia, al - le - lu - ia. Al - le - lu - ia, al - le - lu - ia.

Verse: (Cantor) *to Refrain*

Glory to God___ in the highest, / and on earth peace to those on whom his fav - or rests.

The Nativity of the Lord (Christmas):
At the Mass during the Day

December 25

Psalm 98:1, 2-3, 3-4, 5-6

Gospel Acclamation:

Acclamation: (Keyboard/SATB) NO. V

The Holy Family of Jesus, Mary and Joseph

December 30

(M.M. ♪ = c. 108)

Psalm 84:2-3, 5-6, 9-10

REFRAIN

Bless-ed are they, bless-ed are they, Bless-ed are they who dwell in your house, O Lord.

Verses: (Cantor)

1. How love - ly is your dwell - ing place, / O
2. Hap - py they who dwell in your house! / Con -
3. O LORD_____ of hosts, hear our prayer;

1a. LORD of hosts! My soul yearns and pines
1b. {heart and my flesh cry out
2. tinually they praise you. / Happy the men whose strength you are!
3. hearken, O God of Jacob! / O God, be - hold our shield,

1a. for the courts of the LORD. / My}
1b. for the liv - ing God.
2. Their hearts are set up - on the pilgrimage.
3. and look upon the face of your a - nointed.

a tempo — *to Refrain*

Gospel Acclamation: Acts of the Apostles 16:14b

Acclamation: (Keyboard/SATB) NO. III

(M.M. ♩ = c. 160)

Verse: (Cantor)

to Refrain

Open our hearts, O Lord, / to listen to the words of your Son.

For alternate **Responsorial Psalm** and **Gospel Acclamation Verse,** see *Lectionary for the Mass, Second Typical Edition #17, ABC.*

Solemnity of Mary, the Holy Mother of God

January 1

Gospel Acclamation: Hebrews 1:1-2

Acclamation: (Keyboard/SATB) NO. I

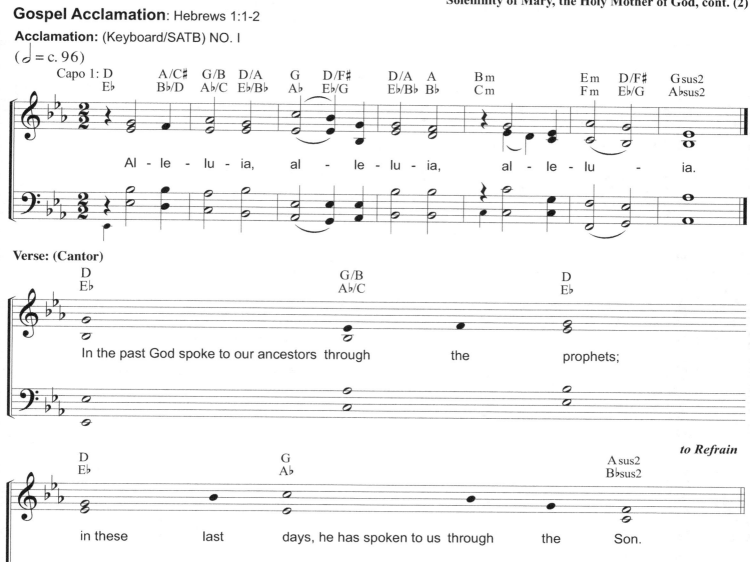

Verse: (Cantor)

In the past God spoke to our ancestors through the prophets;

to Refrain

in these last days, he has spoken to us through the Son.

Music: *Mass of the Sacred Heart*; Timothy R. Smith, © 2007, 2010, Timothy R. Smith. Published by OCP. All rights reserved.

The Epiphany of the Lord

January 6

Psalm 72:1-2, 7-8, 10-11, 12-13

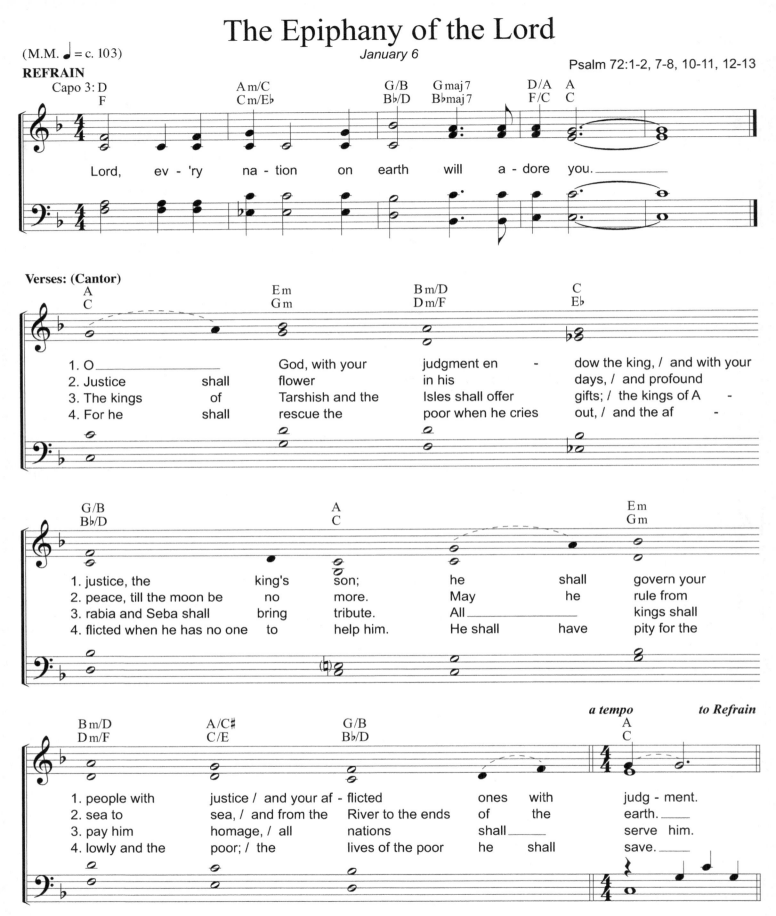

Gospel Acclamation: Matthew 2:2

Acclamation: (Keyboard/SATB) NO. II

(M.M. ♩ = c. 130)

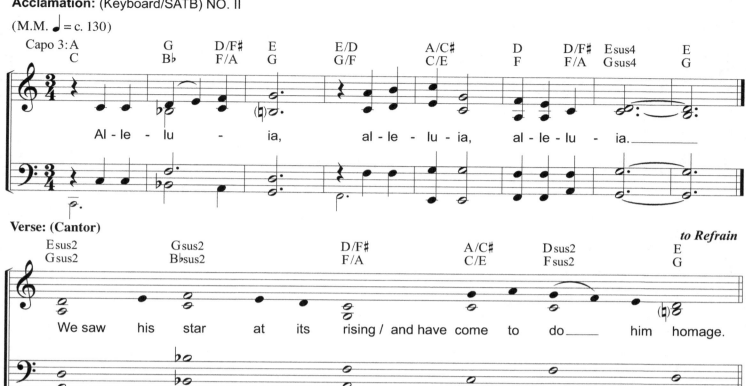

Al - le - lu - ia, al - le - lu - ia, al - le - lu - ia.____

Verse: (Cantor)

to Refrain

We saw his star at its rising / and have come to do____ him homage.

The Baptism of the Lord

January 13

(M.M. ♩ = c. 115)

Psalm 104:1b-2, 3-4, 24-25, 27-28, 29-30

REFRAIN

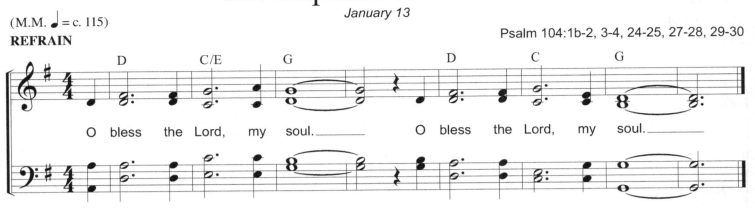

Verses: (Cantor)

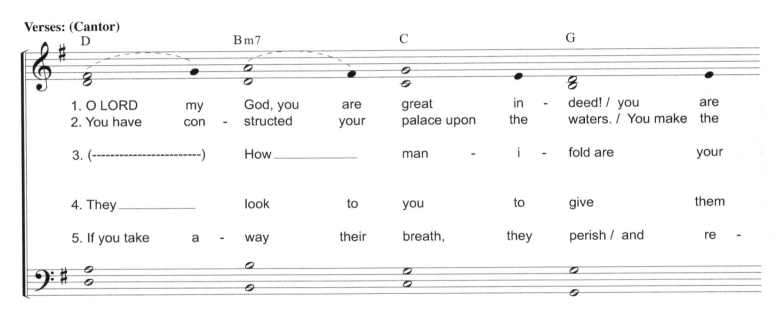

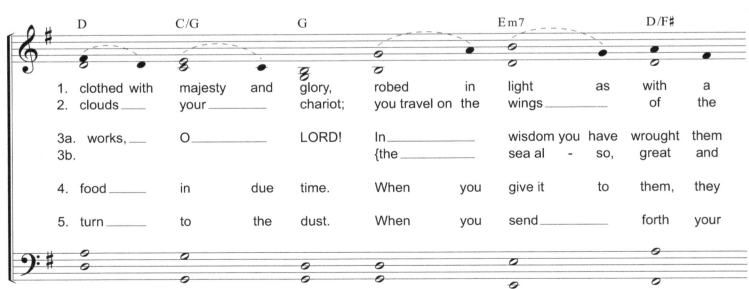

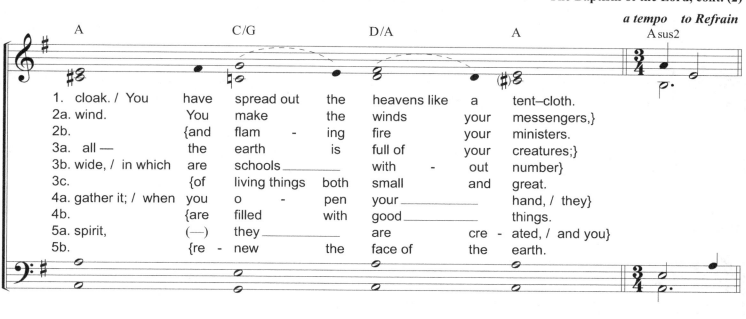

a tempo   to Refrain

	A		C/G		D/A		A		Asus2

1. cloak. / You have spread out the heavens like a tent–cloth.
2a. wind. You make the winds your messengers,}
2b. {and flam - ing fire your ministers.
3a. all — the earth is full of your creatures;}
3b. wide, / in which are schools_____ with - out number}
3c. {of living things both small and great.
4a. gather it; / when you o - pen your_____ hand, / they}
4b. {are filled with good_____ things.
5a. spirit, (—) they_____ are cre - ated, / and you}
5b. {re - new the face of the earth.

Gospel Acclamation: Luke 3:16

Acclamation: (Keyboard/SATB) NO. IV

(M.M. ♩ = c. 116)

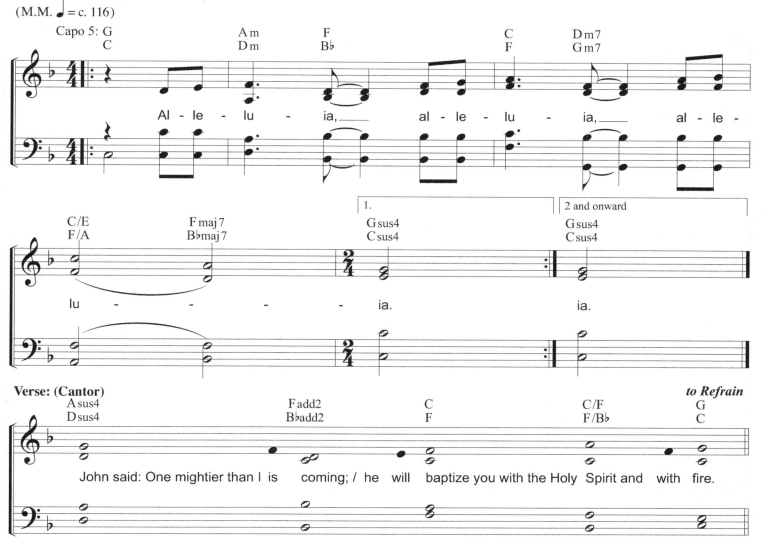

Al - le - lu - ia,____ al - le - lu - ia,____ al - le -

lu - - - - ia. ia.

Verse: (Cantor)

to Refrain

John said: One mightier than I is coming; / he will baptize you with the Holy Spirit and with fire.

For alternate **Responsorial Psalm** and **Gospel Acclamation Verse**, see *Lectionary for the Mass, Second Typical Edition* #21, ABC. 35

Second Sunday in Ordinary Time

January 20

(M.M. ♩= c. 126)

Psalm 96:1-2, 2-3, 7-8, 9-10

REFRAIN

Pro-claim his mar-ve-lous deeds ___ to all ___ the na - tions. ___

Verses: (Cantor)

1. (---) Sing to the LORD a new ___ song; ___
2. An - nounce his sal - vation, day af - ter day. / Tell his
3. (---) Give to the LORD, you fam - 'lies of na - tions,
4a. (---) Wor - ship the LORD in ho - ly at - tire. ___ }
4b. (---) {Trem - ble be - fore him, all ___ the earth; / Say among the

1. sing to the LORD, all you lands. Sing to the
2. glo - ry a - mong ___ the nations; / a - mong all
3. give to the LORD glo - ry and praise; give to the

4b. na - tions, The LORD ___ is king. He ___

1. LORD; ___ bless ___ his name. ___
2. peo - ples, his won - drous deeds. ___
3. LORD ___ the glory due his name! ___

4b. gov - erns the peo - ples with e - qui - ty. ___

a tempo   *to Refrain*

Gospel Acclamation: Thessalonians 2:14

Acclamation: (Keyboard/SATB) NO. IV

(M.M. ♩ = c. 116)

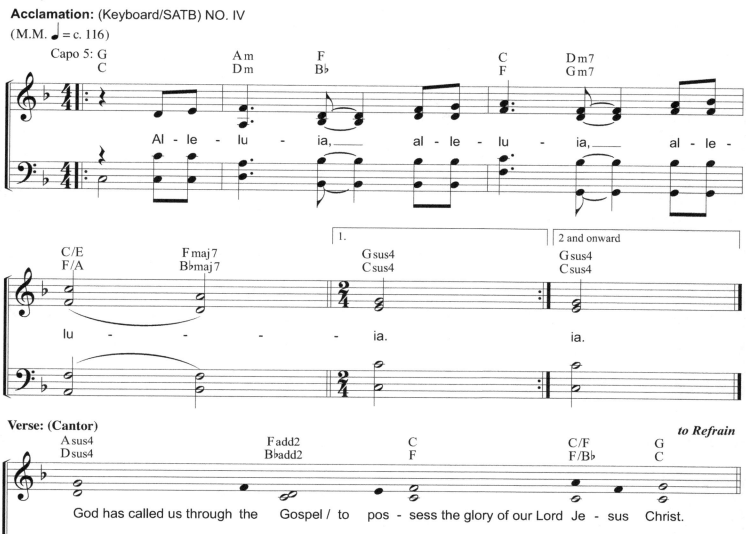

Verse: (Cantor)

to Refrain

God has called us through the Gospel / to pos - sess the glory of our Lord Je - sus Christ.

Third Sunday in Ordinary Time

January 27

Psalm 19:8, 9, 10, 15

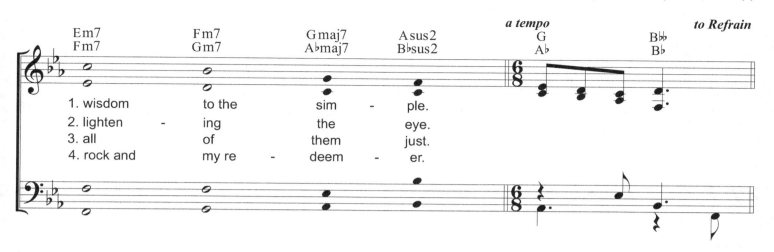

1. wisdom to the sim - ple.
2. lighten - ing the eye.
3. all of them just.
4. rock and my re - deem - er.

Gospel Acclamation: cf. Luke 4:18

Acclamation: (Keyboard/SATB) NO. I

Al - le - lu - ia, al - le - lu - ia, al - le - lu - ia.

Verse: (Cantor)

to Refrain

The Lord sent me to bring glad tidings to the poor, / to pro - claim liber - ty to captives.

Fourth Sunday in Ordinary Time
February 3

www.timothyrsmith.com

Gospel Acclamation: cf. Luke 4:18

Acclamation: (Keyboard/SATB) NO. I

Verse: (Cantor)

to Refrain

The Lord sent me to bring glad tidings to the poor, / to pro - claim liber - ty to captives.

Fifth Sunday in Ordinary Time

February 10

Psalm 138: 1-2, 2-3, 4-5, 7-8

Gospel Acclamation: Matthew 4:19
Acclamation: (Keyboard/SATB) NO. III

Verse: (Cantor)

to Refrain

Sixth Sunday in Ordinary Time

February 17

Psalm 1:1-2, 3, 4 & 6

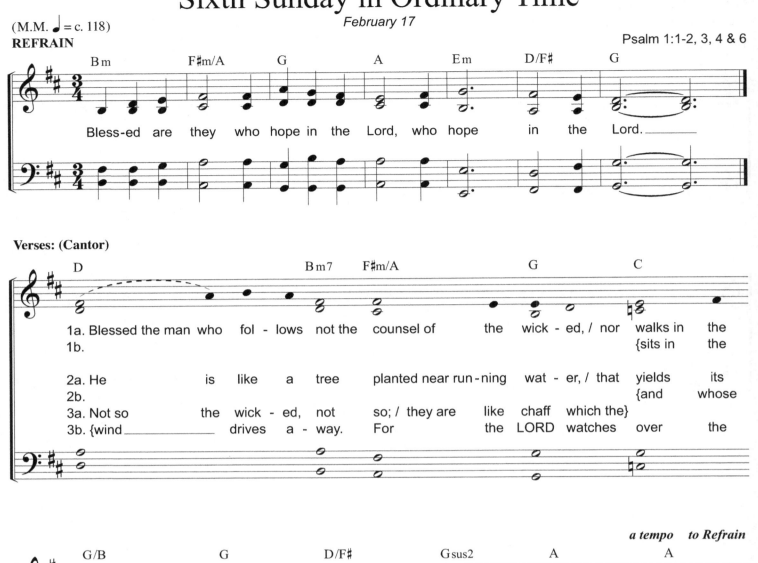

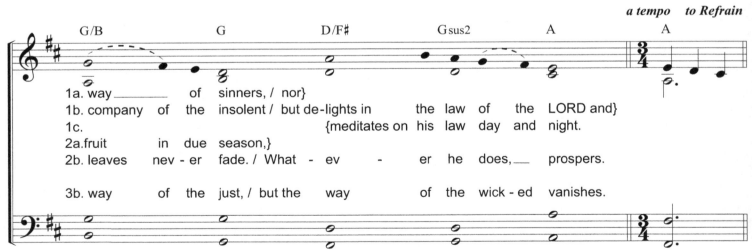

Gospel Acclamation: Luke 6:23ab

Acclamation: (Keyboard/SATB) NO. I

Verse: (Cantor)

Seventh Sunday in Ordinary Time

February 24

Psalm 103:1-2, 3-4, 8, 10, 12-13

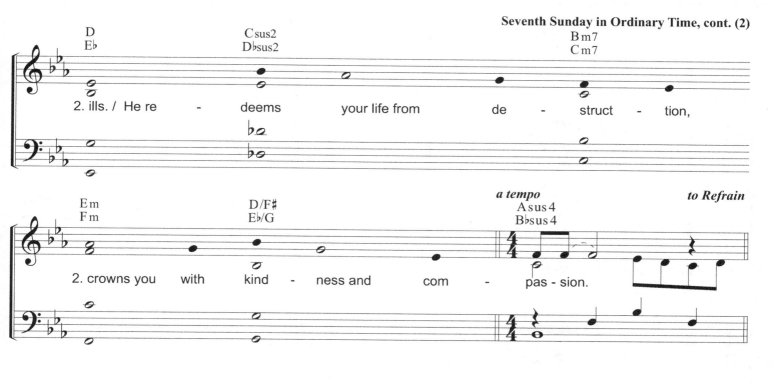

Gospel Acclamation: John 13:34

Acclamation: (Keyboard/SATB) NO. I

Al - le - lu - ia, al - le - lu - ia, al - le - lu - ia.

Verse: (Cantor)

I give you a new commandment, says the Lord: / love one an - other as I have loved you.

Eighth Sunday in Ordinary Time

March 3

Psalm 92:2–3, 13–14, 15–16

NOTE: Refrain Vocals SAB in Treble Clef

a tempo   *to Refrain*

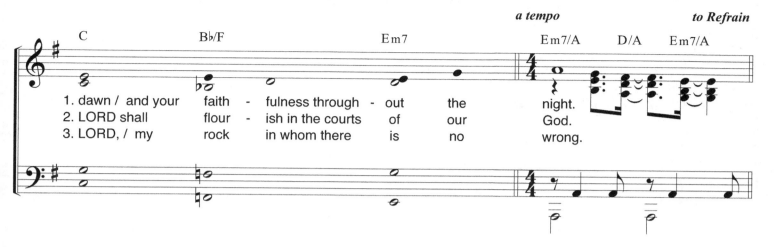

1. dawn / and your faith - fulness through - out the night.
2. LORD shall flour - ish in the courts of our God.
3. LORD, / my rock in whom there is no wrong.

Gospel Acclamation: Philippians 2:15d, 16a

Acclamation: (Keyboard/SATB) NO. I

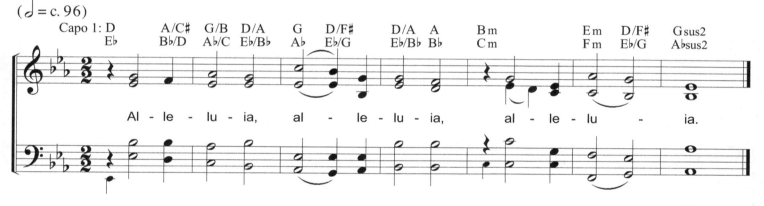

Al - le - lu - ia, al - le - lu - ia, al - le - lu - ia.

Verse: (Cantor)   *to Refrain*

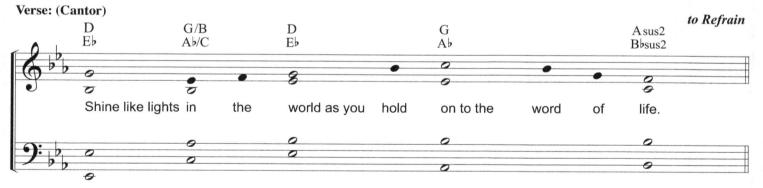

Shine like lights in the world as you hold on to the word of life.

Ash Wednesday

March 6

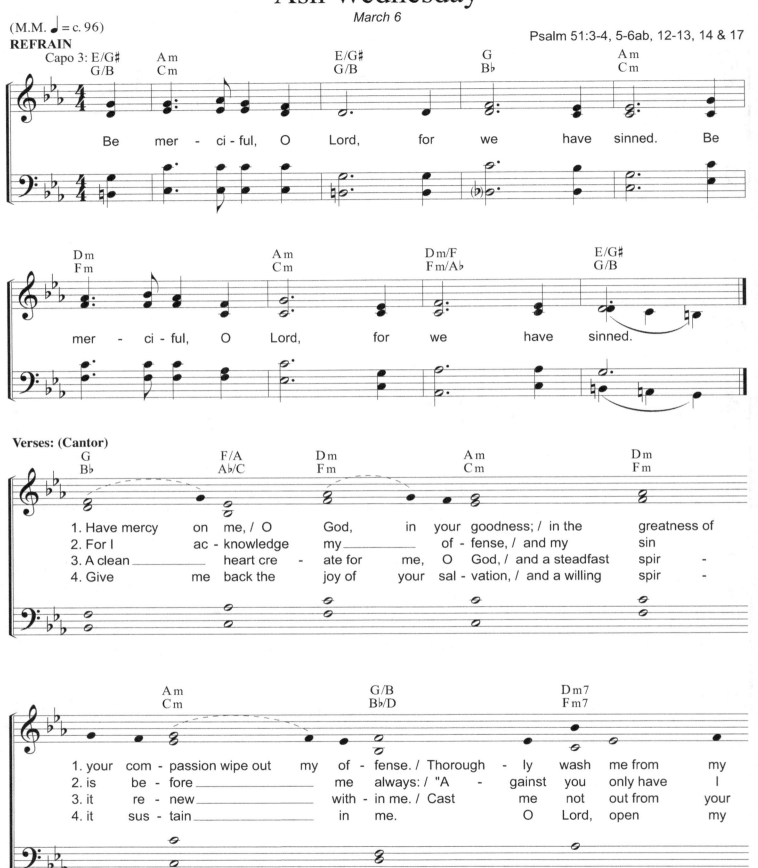

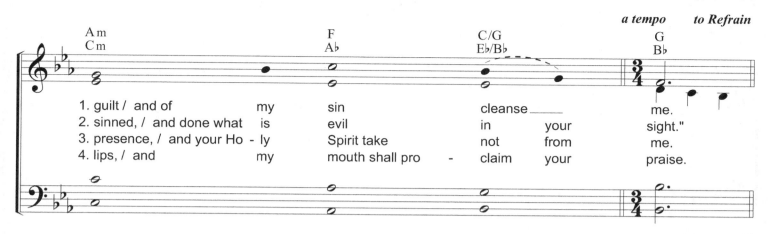

a tempo　　*to Refrain*

1. guilt / and of　　my　　sin　　cleanse_____　　me.
2. sinned, / and done what　is　evil　　in　　your　　sight."
3. presence, / and your Ho - ly　Spirit take　　not　　from　　me.
4. lips, / and　　my　　mouth shall pro - claim　your　　praise.

Gospel Acclamation: Psalm 95:8

Acclamation: (Keyboard/SATB) NO. VII

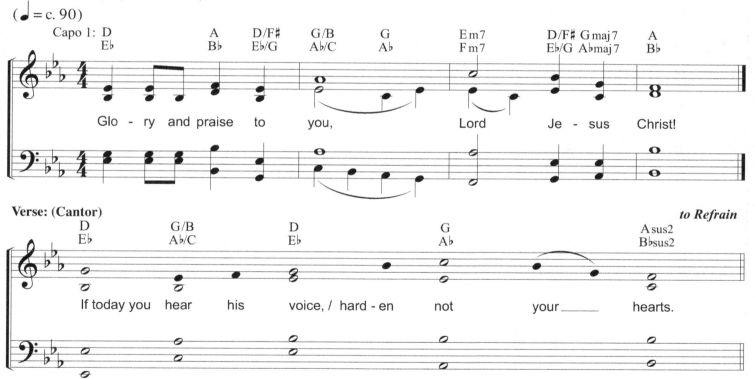

Glo - ry and praise to you, Lord Je - sus Christ!

Verse: (Cantor)　　　　　　　　　　　　　　　*to Refrain*

If today you hear his voice, / hard - en not your_____ hearts.

First Sunday of Lent

March 10

Psalm 91:1-2, 10-11, 12-13, 14-15

www.timothyrsmith.com

Gospel Acclamation: Matthew 4:4b

Acclamation: (Keyboard/SATB) NO. VI

(M.M. ♩ = c. 104)

Praise to you, Lord Je - sus Christ, King of end - less glo - ry!

Verse: (Cantor)

to Refrain

One does not live on bread a - lone, / but on every word that comes forth from the mouth of God.

Second Sunday of Lent

March 17

Psalm 27:1, 7-8, 8-9, 13-14

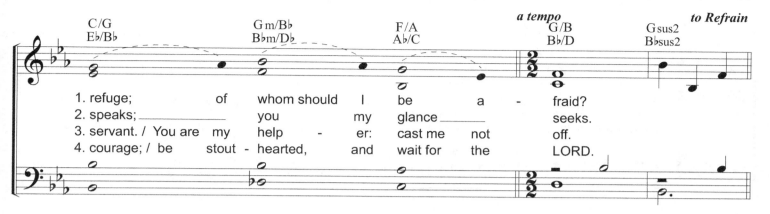

1. refuge; of whom should I be a - fraid?
2. speaks; you my glance seeks.
3. servant. / You are my help - er: cast me not off.
4. courage; / be stout - hearted, and wait for the LORD.

Gospel Acclamation: Matthew 17:5

Acclamation: (Keyboard/SATB) NO. VII

Glo - ry and praise to you, Lord Je - sus Christ!

Verse: (Cantor)

From the shining cloud the Father's voice is heard: / This is my belov - ed Son, hear him.

Third Sunday of Lent
March 24

Psalm 103:1-2, 3-4, 6-7, 8, 11

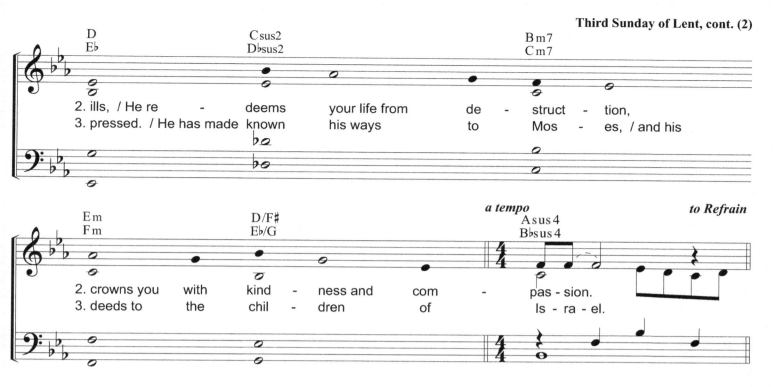

Gospel Acclamation: Matthew 4:17
Acclamation: (Keyboard/SATB) NO. VII

RCIA Option: Third Sunday of Lent

March 24

Gospel Acclamation: cf. John 4:42, 15

Acclamation: (Keyboard/SATB) NO. VI

(M.M. ♩ = c. 104)

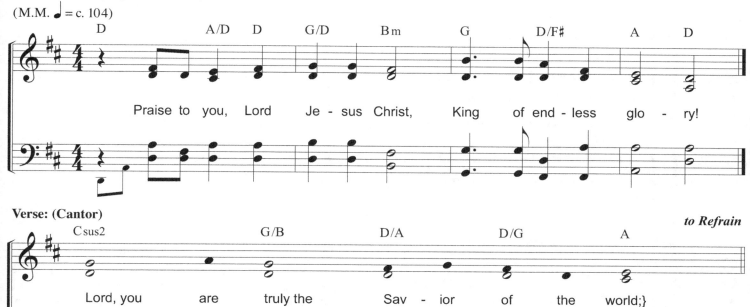

Praise to you, Lord Je - sus Christ, King of end - less glo - ry!

Verse: (Cantor)

to Refrain

Lord, you are truly the Sav - ior of the world;}
{give me liv - ing water, / that I may nev - er thirst a - gain.

Fourth Sunday of Lent

March 31

1. LORD; / the lowly will hear me and be glad._____
2. me / and de - livered me from all my fears._____
3. heard, / and from all his dis - tress he saved him.

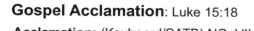

Gospel Acclamation: Luke 15:18

Acclamation: (Keyboard/SATB) NO. VII

(♩ = c. 90)

Glo - ry and praise to you, Lord Je - sus Christ!

Verse: (Cantor) *to Refrain*

I will get up and go to my Father / and}
{shall say to him: / Father I have sinned a - gainst heaven and a - gainst you.

RCIA Option: Fourth Sunday of Lent

March 31

Gospel Acclamation: John 8:12

Acclamation: (Keyboard/SATB) NO. VI

(M.M. ♩ = c. 104)

Praise to you, Lord Je - sus Christ, King of end - less glo - ry!

Verse: (Cantor)

to Refrain

I am the light of the world, says the Lord; / whoever follows me will have the light of life.

Music © 2014, Timothy R. Smith. Published by TR TUNE, LLC. All rights reserved.

Fifth Sunday of Lent

April 7

Psalm 126:1-2, 2-3, 4-5, 6

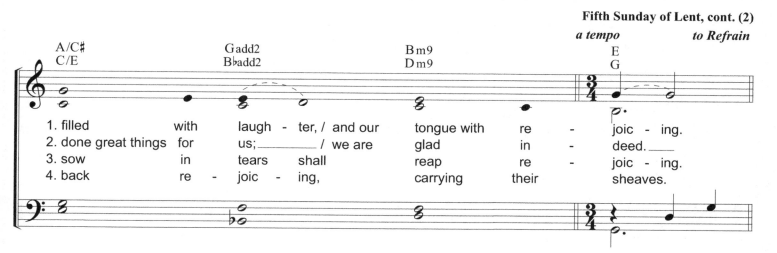

1. filled with laugh - ter, / and our tongue with re - joic - ing.
2. done great things for us;_____ / we are glad in - deed.____
3. sow in tears shall reap re - joic - ing.
4. back re - joic - ing, carrying their sheaves.

Gospel Acclamation: Joel 2:12-13

Acclamation: (Keyboard/SATB) NO. VII

(♩ = c. 90)

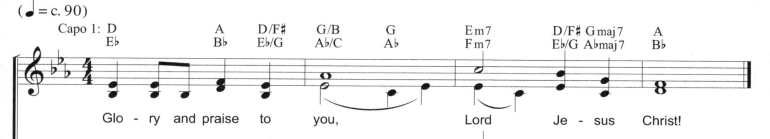

Glo - ry and praise to you, Lord Je - sus Christ!

Verse: (Cantor) *to Refrain*

Even now, says the Lord, / re-turn to me with your whole heart; / for I am gra - cious and merciful.

RCIA Option: Fifth Sunday of Lent

April 7

Gospel Acclamation: John 11:25a, 26

Acclamation: (Keyboard/SATB) NO. VI

(M.M. ♩ = c. 104)

Praise to you, Lord Je-sus Christ, King of end-less glo-ry!

Verse: (Cantor)

to Refrain

I am the resurrection and the life, says the Lord; / whoever be-lieves____ in____ me,}
{even if he dies, will____ nev-er die.

Music © 2014, Timothy R. Smith. Published by TR TUNE, LLC. All rights reserved.

Palm Sunday of the Passion of the Lord

April 14

(M.M. ♩ = c. 92)

Psalm 22:8-9, 17-18, 19-20, 23-24

Gospel Acclamation: Philippians 2:8-9
Acclamation: (Keyboard/SATB) NO. VII

Verse: (Cantor)

Thursday of the Lord's Supper (Holy Thursday):
At the Evening Mass
April 18

Psalm 116:12-13,15-16bc, 17-18

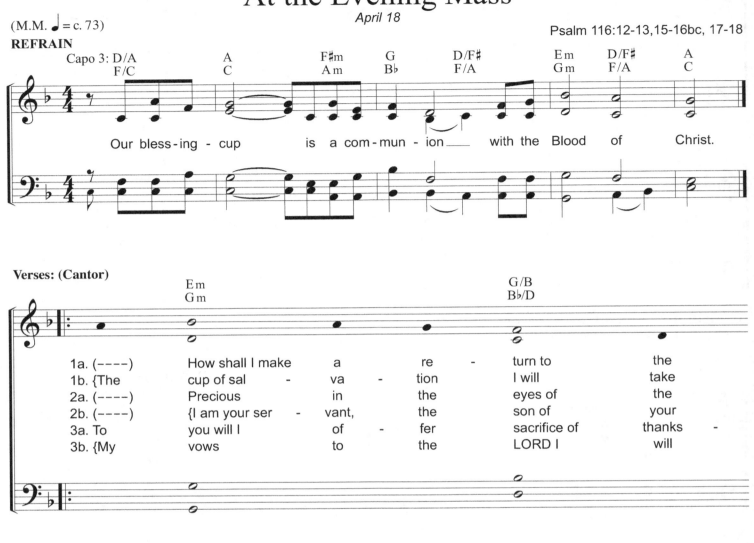

Our bless-ing - cup is a com-mun - ion___ with the Blood of Christ.

Verses: (Cantor)

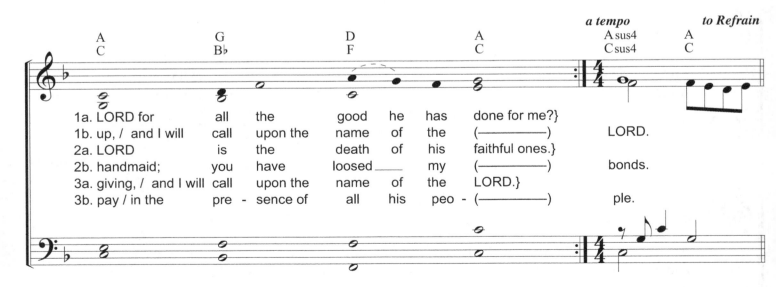

1a. (----) How shall I make a re - turn to the
1b. {The cup of sal - va - tion I will take
2a. (----) Precious in the eyes of the
2b. (----) {I am your ser - vant, the son of your
3a. To you will I of - fer sacrifice of thanks -
3b. {My vows to the LORD I will

1a. LORD for all the good he has done for me?}
1b. up, / and I will call upon the name of the (————) LORD.
2a. LORD is the death of his faithful ones.}
2b. handmaid; you have loosed___ my (————) bonds.
3a. giving, / and I will call upon the name of the LORD.}
3b. pay / in the pre - sence of all his peo - (————) ple.

Gospel Acclamation: John 13:34

Acclamation: (Keyboard/SATB) NO. VII

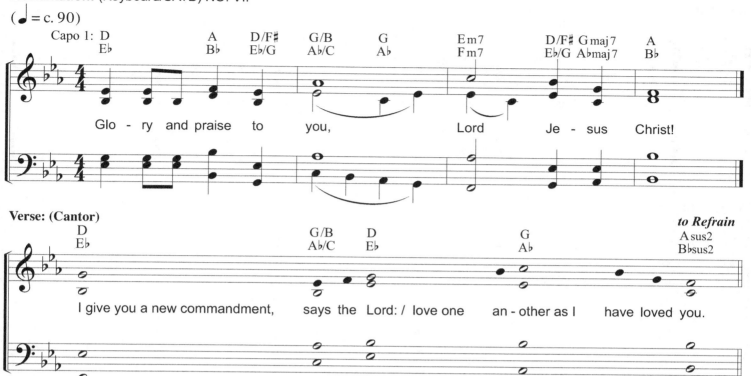

Glo - ry and praise to you, Lord Je - sus Christ!

Verse: (Cantor)

to Refrain

I give you a new commandment, says the Lord: / love one an - other as I have loved you.

Music: *Mass of the Sacred Heart*; Timothy R. Smith, © 2007, 2010, Timothy R. Smith. Published by OCP. All rights reserved.

Friday of the Passion of the Lord (Good Friday)

(M.M. ♩ = c. 94)

April 19

Psalm 31:2, 6, 12-13, 15-16, 17, 25

Gospel Acclamation: Philippians 2:8-9

Acclamation: (Keyboard/SATB) NO. VII

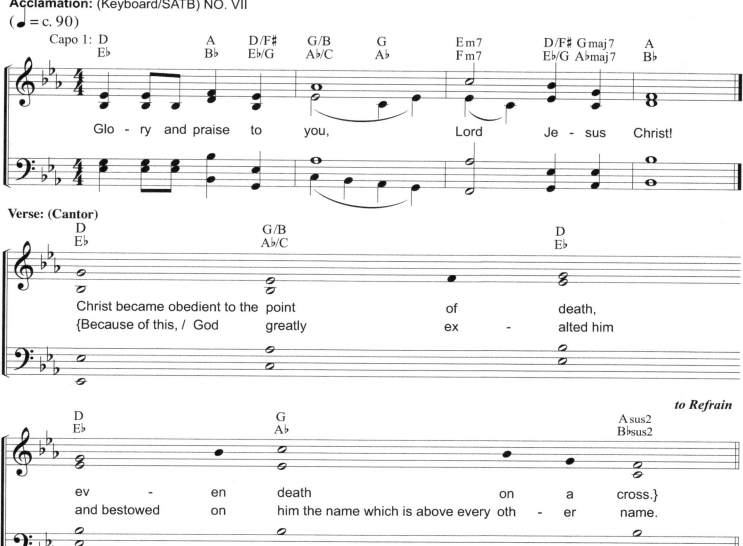

The Easter Vigil in the Holy Night

Responsorial Psalm (following first reading) *April 20*

(M.M. ♩ = c. 115)

Psalm 104:1-2, 5-6, 10, 12, 13-14, 24, 35

Alternate Responsorial Psalm (Following first reading)

Psalm 33:4-5, 6-7, 12-13, 20 & 22

Responsorial Psalm (following second reading)

(M.M. ♩ = c. 105)

Psalm 16:5, 8, 9-10,11

REFRAIN

You are my in-her-i-tance, you are my in-her-i-tance, O Lord.

Verses: (Cantor)

1. O LORD, my al-lot-ted portion and my cup, you it is who hold fast my lot. I set the LORD ev-er be-
2. Therefore my heart is glad and my soul re-joices, / my bod-y, too, a-bides in confidence; / because you will not a-bandon my soul to the
3. You will show me the path to life, full-ness of joys in your presence, / the de-lights at your right hand for-

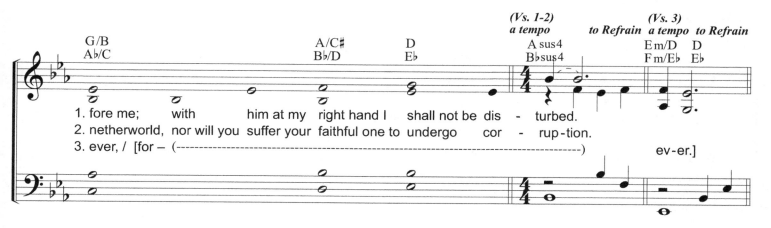

1. fore me; with him at my right hand I shall not be dis - turbed.
2. netherworld, nor will you suffer your faithful one to undergo cor - rup-tion.
3. ever, / [for – (--) ev-er.]

The Easter Vigil in the Holy Night, cont.
Responsorial Psalm (following third reading)

(M.M. ♩ = c. 102)

Exodus 15:1-2, 3-4, 5-6, 17-18

REFRAIN

Let us sing to the Lord; he has cov-ered him-self in glo - ry.

Verse 1: (Cantor)

1. I will sing to the LORD, for he is glori - ous - ly tri - umphant; horse and chariot he has

1a. cast in - to the sea. My strength and my cour - age is_____ the
1b.   {my God,_____ I

1a. LORD,   and   he has   been   my   sav - ior. / He is}
1b. praise him; / the God of my   father,   I   ex - tol   him.

a tempo   to Refrain

Verses 2 & 3: (Cantor)

2. The LORD is a   war - rior,   LORD   is_____   his   name!
3. The flood waters cov - ered them, / they sank into the   depths   like   a   stone.

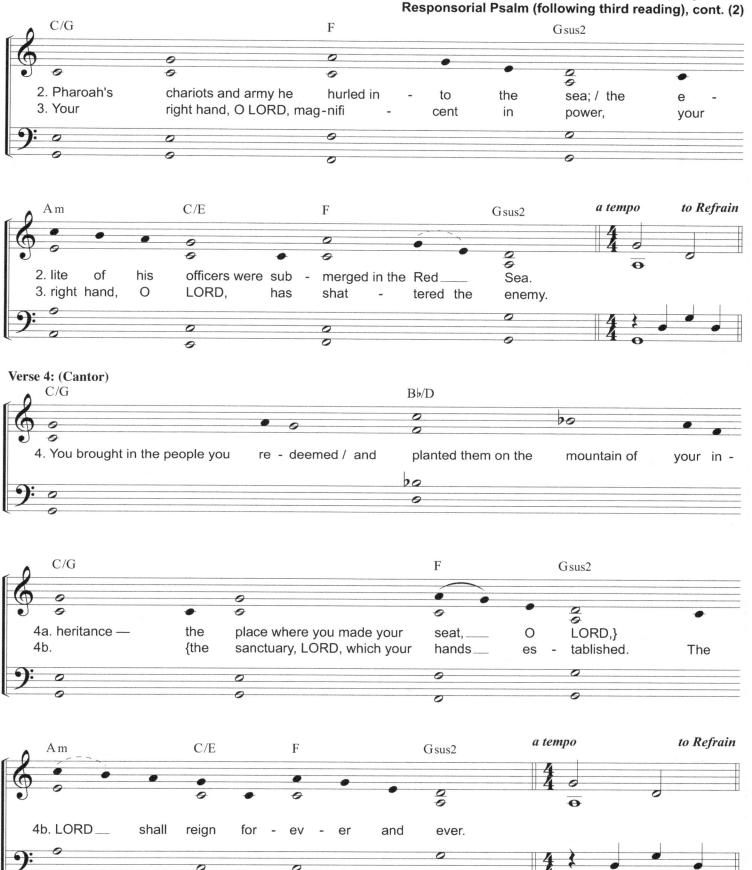

Verse 4: (Cantor)

2. Pharoah's chariots and army he hurled in - to the sea; / the e -
3. Your right hand, O LORD, mag-nifi - cent in power, your

2. lite of his officers were sub - merged in the Red____ Sea.
3. right hand, O LORD, has shat - tered the enemy.

4. You brought in the people you re - deemed / and planted them on the mountain of your in -

4a. heritage — the place where you made your seat,___ O LORD,}
4b. {the sanctuary, LORD, which your hands___ es - tablished. The

4b. LORD___ shall reign for - ev - er and ever.

Responsorial Psalm (following fourth reading)

(M.M. ♩ = c. 118)

REFRAIN

Psalm 30:2, 4, 5-6, 11-12, 13

I will praise you, ___ Lord, for you have res - cued me.

Verses: (Cantor)

1. I will ex - tol you, O LORD, for you drew me clear and did
2. Sing ___ praise to the LORD, / you his faith - ful ones, / and give
3. Hear, O LORD, and have pity, [have pity] on me; / O, (—)

1. not let my enemies re - joice ov - er me. O ___
2. thanks ___ to his ho - ly name. For his
3. (———————) LORD, ___ be my helper. You ___

1. LORD, you brought me up from the neth - er - world; / you pre -
2. anger lasts but a moment; / a lifetime, his good will. / At
3. changed my mourning in - to dancing; / O LORD, ___ my God, / for -

1. served me from a - mong those going down in - to the pit.
2. nightfall, weeping en - ters in, / but with the dawn, ___ re - joicing.
3. ev - er will I give ___ you thanks.

a tempo **to Refrain**

Responsorial Psalm (following fifth reading)

(M.M. ♩ = c. 120)

REFRAIN

Isaiah 12:2-3, 4, 5-6

Verses: (Cantor)

1a. God in - deed is my savior; / I am confident and un - a - fraid.}
1b. {My strength and my courage is the LORD, and he has been my savior.
2a. Give thanks to the LORD, ac - claim his name;}
2b. {a - mong the nations make known his deeds,
3a. Sing praise to the LORD for his glorious a - chievement;}
3b. {let this be known through - out all the earth.}
3c. {Shout with ex - ul - tation, O city of Zion,

a tempo   *to Refrain*

1b. With joy you will draw wa - ter at the fountain of sal - vation.

2b. pro - claim how ex - alt - ed is his name.

3c. for great in your midst is the Holy One of Israel!

www.timothyrsmith.com

The Easter Vigil in the Holy Night, cont.

Responsorial Psalm (following sixth reading)

(M.M. ♩ = c. 118)

REFRAIN

Psalm 19:8, 9, 10, 11

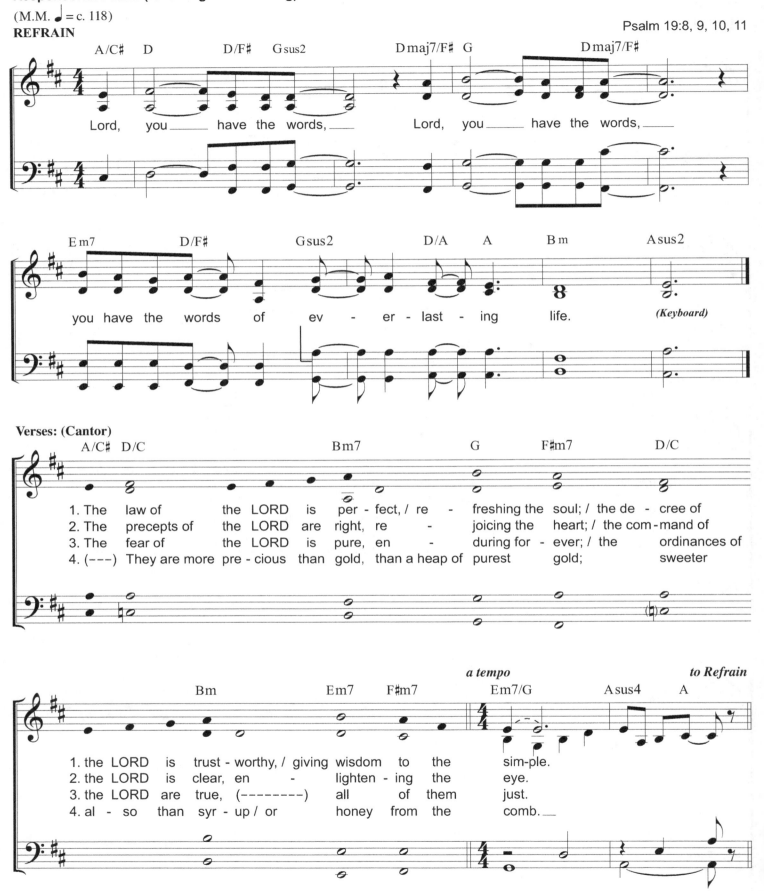

Option A, when Baptism is celebrated
Responsorial Psalm (following seventh reading)

(M.M. ♩ = c. 68)

REFRAIN

Psalm 42:3, 5; 43:3, 4

Verses: (Cantor)

Or: Option B, when Baptism is not celebrated
Responsorial Psalm (following seventh reading)

(M.M. ♩ = c. 120)
REFRAIN

Isaiah 12:2-3, 4bcd, 5-6

You will draw wat - er joy - ful - ly _____ from the springs of _____ sal - va - tion. _____

Verses: (Cantor)

1a. God in - deed is my savior; / I am confident and un - a - fraid.}
1b. {My strength and my courage is the LORD, and he has been my savior.
2a. Give _____ thanks to the LORD, ac - claim his name;}
2b. {a - mong the nations make known his deeds,
3a. Sing _____ praise to the LORD for his glorious a - chievement;}
3b. {let _____ this be known through - out all the earth.}
3c. {Shout with ex - ul - tation, O city of Zion,

a tempo   *to Refrain*

1b. With joy you will draw wa - ter at the fountain of sal - vation.

2b. pro - claim how ex - alt - ed is his name.

3c. for great in your midst is the Holy One of Israel!

Or: Option C, when Baptism is not celebrated
Responsorial Psalm (following seventh reading)

Psalm 51:12-13, 14-15, 18-19

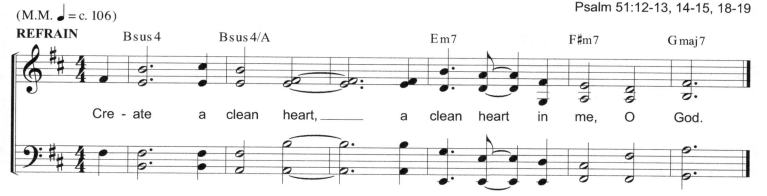

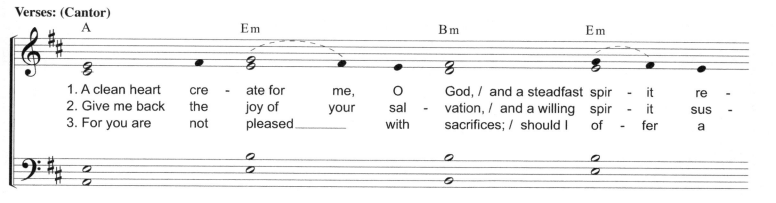

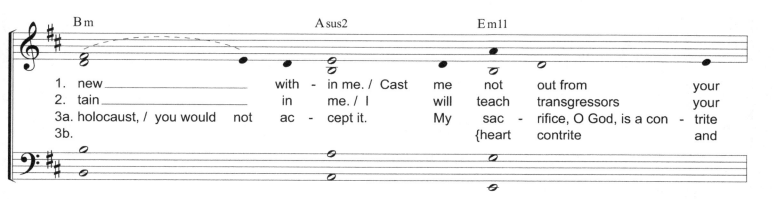

Responsorial Psalm: Psalm 118:1-2, 16-17, 22-23

Acclamation: (Keyboard/SATB) NO. II

Easter Sunday of the Resurrection of the Lord:
At the Mass during the Day

April 21

Psalm 118:1-2, 16-17, 22-23

Gospel Acclamation: cf. 1 Corinthians 5:7b-8a

Acclamation: (Keyboard/SATB) NO. V

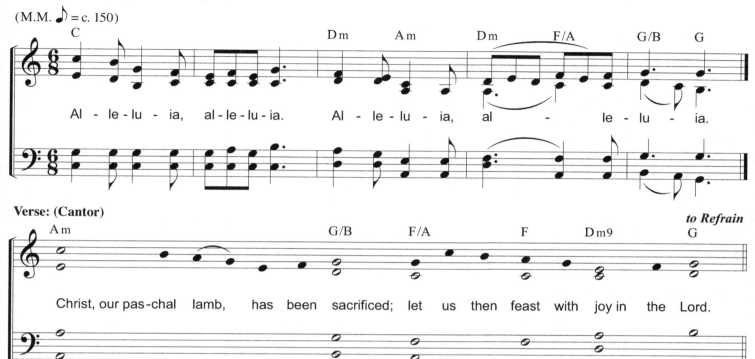

Verse: (Cantor)

to Refrain

Christ, our pas-chal lamb, has been sacrificed; let us then feast with joy in the Lord.

Second Sunday of Easter (or Sunday of Divine Mercy)

April 28

(M.M. ♩ = c. 100)

Psalm 118:2-4, 13-15, 22-24

REFRAIN [or: Alleluia]

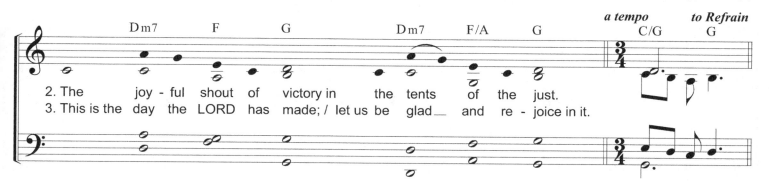

2. The joy - ful shout of victory in the tents of the just.
3. This is the day the LORD has made; / let us be glad___ and re - joice in it.

Gospel Acclamation: John 20:29

Acclamation: (Keyboard/SATB) NO. III

(M.M. ♩ = c. 160)

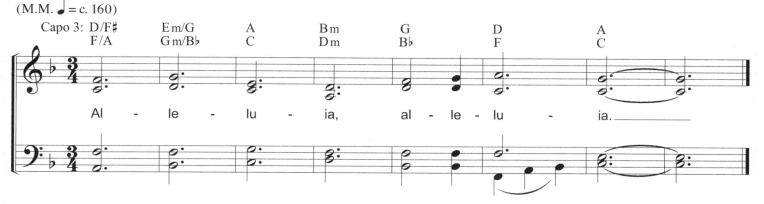

Al - le - lu - ia, al - le - lu - ia.___

Verse: (Cantor)

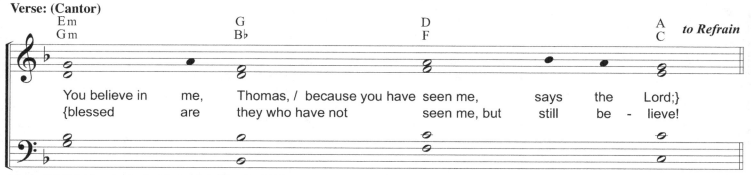

You believe in me, Thomas, / because you have seen me, says the Lord;}
{blessed are they who have not seen me, but still be - lieve!

Third Sunday of Easter
May 5

Gospel Acclamation:

Acclamation: (Keyboard/SATB) NO. III

(M.M. ♩ = c. 160)

Al - le - lu - ia, al - le - lu - ia._____

Verse: (Cantor)

Christ is risen, / cre - a - tor of all;}
{he has shown pity on all_____ people.

to Refrain

Fourth Sunday of Easter

May 12

Psalm 100:1-2, 3, 5

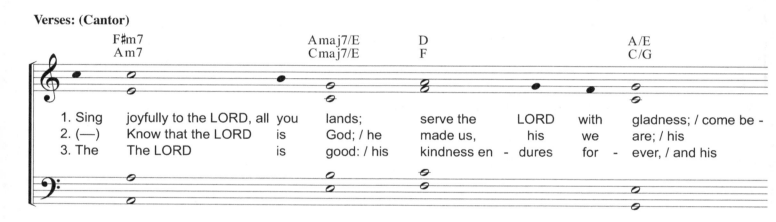

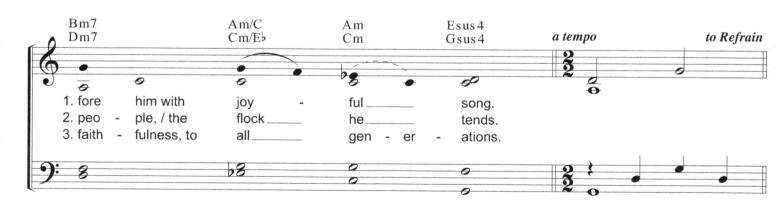

Gospel Acclamation: John 10:14

Acclamation: (Keyboard/SATB) NO. IV

(M.M. ♩ = c. 116)

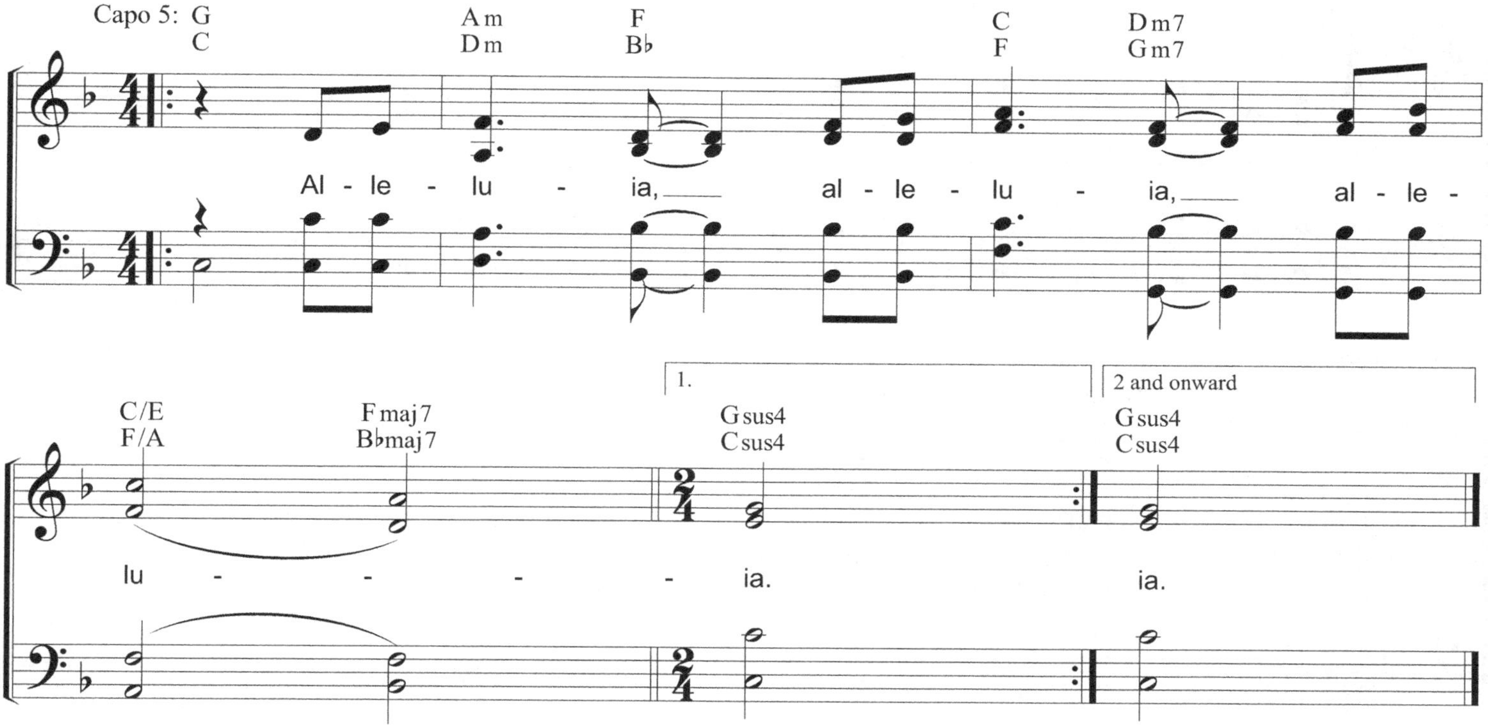

Capo 5: G C
Am Dm
F B♭
C F
Dm7 Gm7
C/E F/A
Fmaj7 B♭maj7
1.
Gsus4 Csus4
2 and onward
Gsus4 Csus4
Al - le - lu - ia, al - le - lu - ia, al - le - lu - ia.
ia.

Verse: (Cantor)

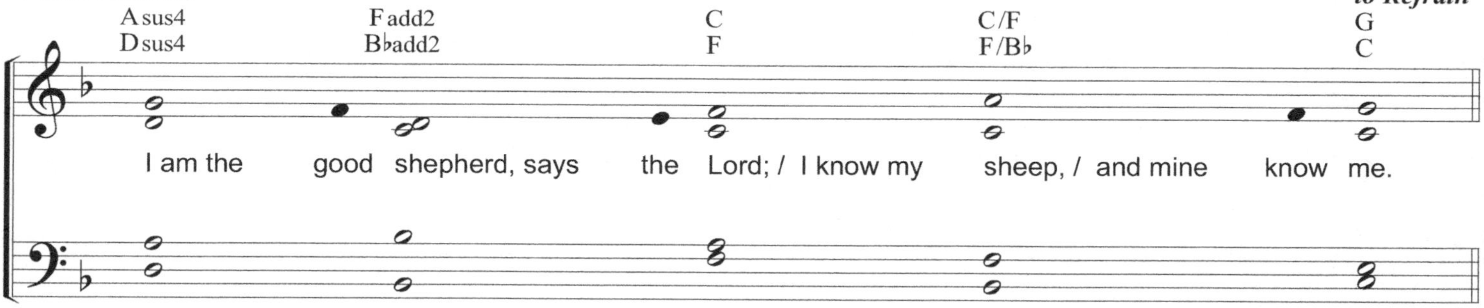

Asus4 Dsus4
Fadd2 B♭add2
C F
C/F F/B♭
to Refrain
G C
I am the good shepherd, says the Lord; / I know my sheep, / and mine know me.

Fifth Sunday of Easter

May 19

Psalm 145:8-9, 10-11, 12-13

Gospel Acclamation: John 13:34

Acclamation: (Keyboard/SATB) NO. I

(♩ = c. 96)

Al - le - lu - ia, al - le - lu - ia, al - le - lu - ia.

Verse: (Cantor)

to Refrain

I give you a new commandment, says the Lord: / love one an - other as I have loved you.

Sixth Sunday of Easter
May 26

Psalm 67:2-3, 5, 6, 8

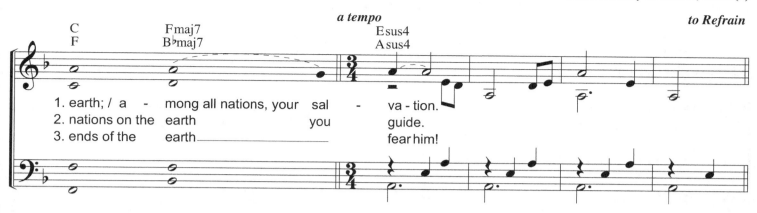

a tempo

to Refrain

1. earth; / a - mong all nations, your sal - va - tion.
2. nations on the earth you guide.
3. ends of the earth fear him!

Gospel Acclamation: John 14:23

Acclamation: (Keyboard/SATB) NO. II

(M.M. ♩ = c. 130)

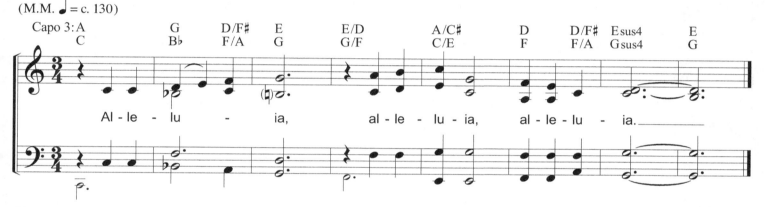

Al - le - lu - ia, al - le - lu - ia, al - le - lu - ia.

Verse: (Cantor)

Whoever loves me will keep my word, says the Lord, / and my

Father will love him / and we will come to him.

to Refrain

The Ascension of the Lord

May 30 or June 2

The Ascension of the Lord may be celebrated on May 30 or transferred
to June 2, depending upon the practice of each province.

Gospel Acclamation: Matthew 28:19a, 20b
Acclamation: (Keyboard/SATB) NO. III

(M.M. ♩ = c. 160)

Capo 3: D/F♯   Em/G   A   Bm   G   D   A
F/A   Gm/B♭   C   Dm   B♭   F   C

Al – le – lu – ia, al – le – lu – ia._____

Verse: (Cantor)

Em   G   D   A
Gm   B♭   F   C   *to Refrain*

Go   and   teach all   nations,   says   the   Lord;}
{I am with   you   always, / until the   end   of   the   world.

Seventh Sunday of Easter

June 2

7th Sunday of Easter may be replaced by *The Ascension of the Lord* (pp. 100-101),
depending upon the practice of each province.

Psalm 97:1-2, 6-7, 9

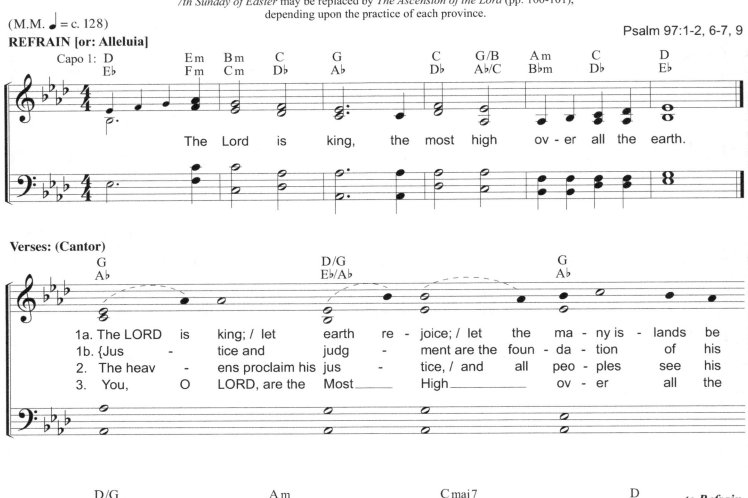

REFRAIN [or: Alleluia]

The Lord is king, the most high ov-er all the earth.

Verses: (Cantor)

1a. The LORD is king; / let earth re-joice; / let the ma-ny is-lands be
1b. {Jus - tice and judg - ment are the foun-da-tion of his
2. The heav - ens proclaim his jus - tice, / and all peo-ples see his
3. You, O LORD, are the Most High ov-er all the

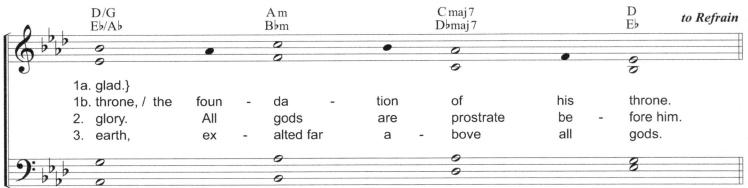

1a. glad.}
1b. throne, / the foun - da - tion of his throne.
2. glory. All gods are prostrate be - fore him.
3. earth, ex - alted far a - bove all gods.

to Refrain

Gospel Acclamation: cf. John 14:18

Acclamation: (Keyboard/SATB) NO. IV

(M.M. ♩ = c. 116)

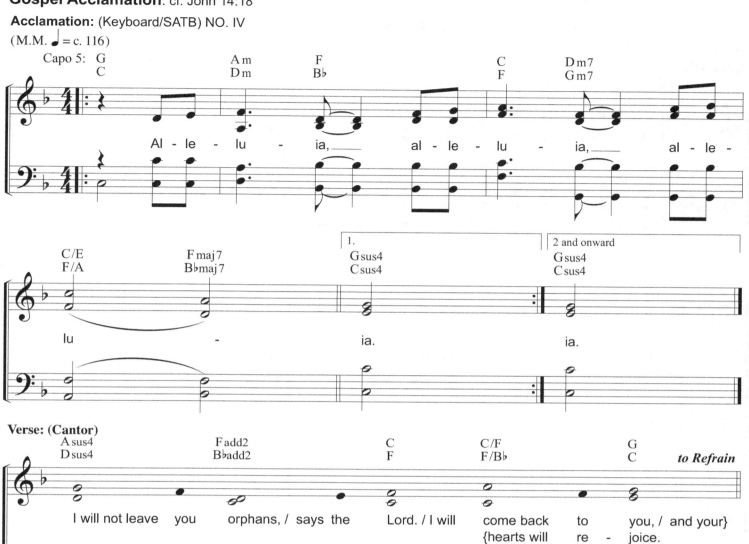

Verse: (Cantor)

I will not leave you orphans, / says the Lord. / I will come back to you, / and your}
{hearts will re - joice.

Pentecost Sunday: At the Vigil Mass
(Extended Form)
June 8

Psalm 33:10-11, 12-13, 14-15

Option 1:

Responsorial Psalm (following second reading)

(M.M. ♩ = c. 72)

Daniel 3:52, 53, 54, 55, 56

Verses 1-2: (Cantor)

1a. "Blessed are you, O Lord, the God of our fathers, praise - worthy
1b. {and_____ blessed is your holy and glo - rious name, praise - worthy
2. "Blessed are you in the temple of your ho - ly glory, praise - worthy

a tempo *to Refrain*

1a. and ex - alt - ed a - bove___ all for - ev - er;}
1b. and ex - alt - ed a - bove all for all a - ges."
2. and glo - ri - ous a - bove___ all for - ev - er."

Verses 3-5: (Cantor)

3. "Blessed are you on the throne of your King - dom, (--------------------------------------)
4. "Blessed are you who look in - to the depths from your throne up-on the cher - ubim,
5. "Blessed are you in the firma - ment of heav - en, (--------------------------------------)

Through composed octavo Ed. 21021, available at www.ocp.org

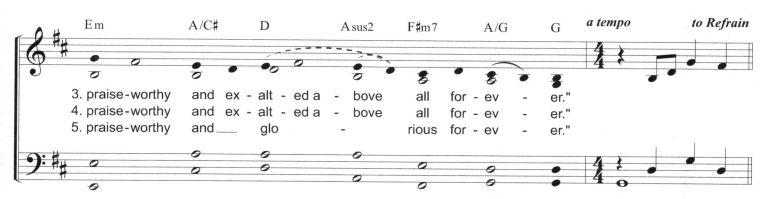

3. praise-worthy and ex - alt - ed a - bove all for - ev - er."
4. praise-worthy and ex - alt - ed a - bove all for - ev - er."
5. praise-worthy and___ glo - rious for - ev - er."

Responsorial Psalm (following second reading)

(M.M. ♩ = c. 118)   Psalm 19:8, 9, 10, 11

REFRAIN

Lord, you have the words, Lord, you have the words, you have the words of ev - er - last - ing life. *(Keyboard)*

Verses: (Cantor)

1. The law of the LORD is per - fect, / re - freshing the soul; / the de - cree of
2. The precepts of the LORD are right, re - joicing the heart; / the com - mand of
3. The fear of the LORD is pure, en - during for - ev - er; / the ordinances of
4. (---) They are more pre - cious than gold, than a heap of purest gold; sweeter

a tempo   *to Refrain*

1. the LORD is trust - worthy, / giving wisdom to the sim - ple.
2. the LORD is clear, en - lighten - ing the eye.
3. the LORD are true, (--------) all of them just.
4. al - so than syr - up / or honey from the comb.

(M.M. ♩ = c. 132)

Psalm 107:2-3, 4-5, 6-7, 8-9

REFRAIN [or: Alleluia]

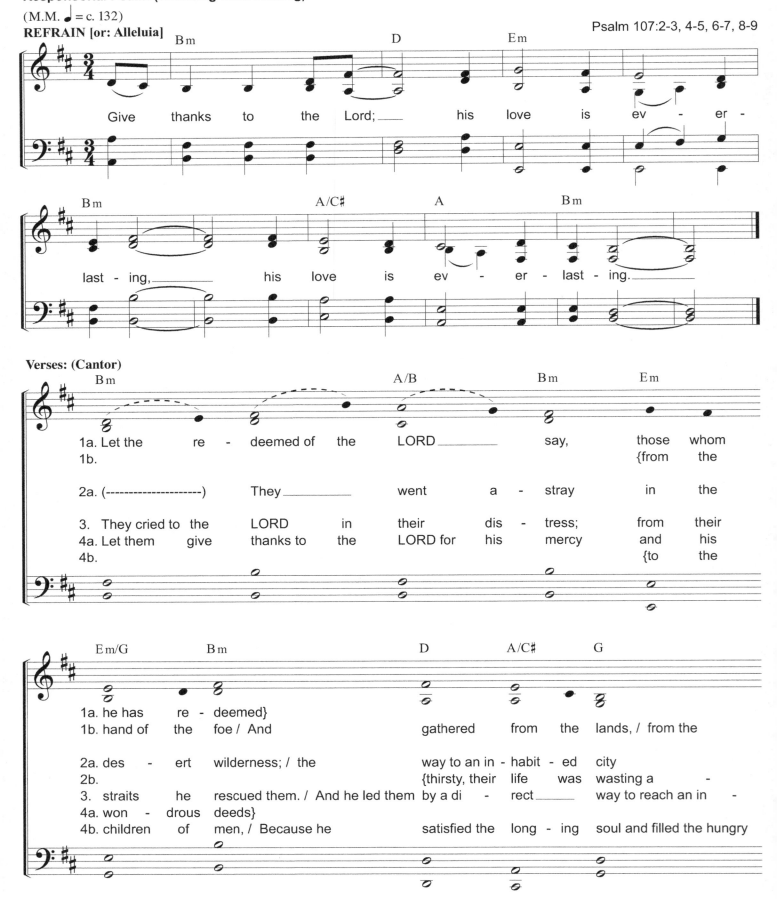

Verses: (Cantor)

1a. Let the re - deemed of the LORD ____ say, those whom
1b. {from the

2a. (---------------------) They ____ went a - stray in the

3. They cried to the LORD in their dis - tress; from their
4a. Let them give thanks to the LORD for his mercy and his
4b. {to the

1a. he has re - deemed}
1b. hand of the foe / And gathered from the lands, / from the

2a. des - ert wilderness; / the way to an in - habit - ed city
2b. {thirsty, their life was wasting a -
3. straits he rescued them. / And he led them by a di - rect ____ way to reach an in -
4a. won - drous deeds}
4b. children of men, / Because he satisfied the long - ing soul and filled the hungry

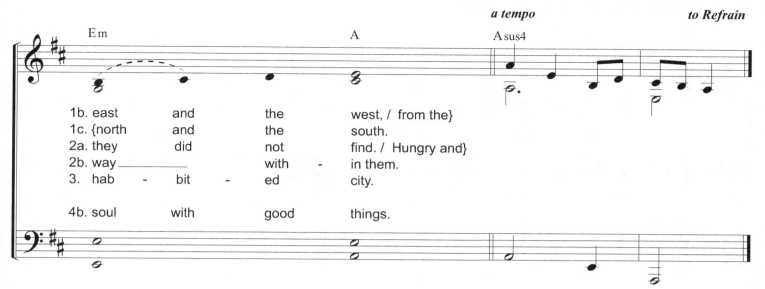

1b. east   and   the   west, / from the}
1c. {north   and   the   south.
2a. they   did   not   find. / Hungry and}
2b. way _____   with -   in them.
3. hab -   bit -   ed   city.

4b. soul   with   good   things.

(M.M. ♩ = c. 115)

Psalm 104:1-2, 24 & 35, 27-28, 29-30

REFRAIN [or: Alleluia]

Lord, send out your Spir - it, and re-new the face of the earth.

Verses: (Cantor)

1. Bless the LORD, O my soul! / O LORD, my God, you are
2. (--------------------) How man - i - fold are your works,

3. Crea - tures all look to you to give them
4. If you take a - way their breath, they perish / and re - turn

1. great in - deed! You are clothed with majesty and
2. O LORD! In wisdom you have wrought them

3. food in due time. When you give it to them, they
4. to their dust. When you send forth your

a tempo *to Refrain*

1. glory, / robed in light as with a cloak.
2a. all – the earth is full of your creatures; / bless}
2b. {the LORD, O my soul!}
2c. {Al - le - lu - ia.
3. gather it; / when you open your hand, they are filled with good things.
4a. spir - it, they are cre - ated, / and you}
4b. {re - new the face of the earth.

Gospel Acclamation:

Acclamation: (Keyboard/SATB) NO. V

(M.M. ♪ = c. 150)

Al - le -lu - ia, al -le -lu - ia. Al - le -lu - ia, al - le - lu - ia.

Verse: (Cantor)

to Refrain

Come, Holy Spirit, fill the hearts of your faithful / and kin - dle in them the fire of your love.

Pentecost Sunday: At the Mass during the Day

June 9

Gospel Acclamation:

Acclamation: (Keyboard/SATB) NO. V

(M.M. ♪ = c. 150)

Al - le -lu - ia, al -le -lu - ia. Al - le - lu - ia, al - le - lu - ia.

Verse: (Cantor)

to Refrain

Come, Holy Spirit, fill the hearts of your faithful / and kin - dle in them the fire of your love.

The Most Holy Trinity

June 16

a tempo   *to Refrain*

1. son of man that you _____ should care for him?
2. put - ting all things un - der his feet.
3. ev - er swims the paths of the seas.

Gospel Acclamation: cf. Revelation 1:8

Acclamation: (Keyboard/SATB) NO. I

Al - le - lu - ia, al - le - lu - ia, al - le - lu - ia.

Verse: (Cantor)

to Refrain

Glory to the Father, the Son, and the Ho - ly Spirit: / to God who is, who was, / and who is to come.

The Most Holy Body and
Blood of Christ (Corpus Christi)

June 23

(M.M. ♩ = c. 88)

Psalm 110:1, 2, 3, 4

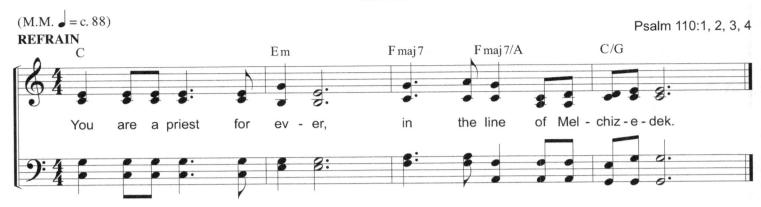

REFRAIN

You are a priest for ev - er, in the line of Mel - chiz - e - dek.

Verses: (Cantor)

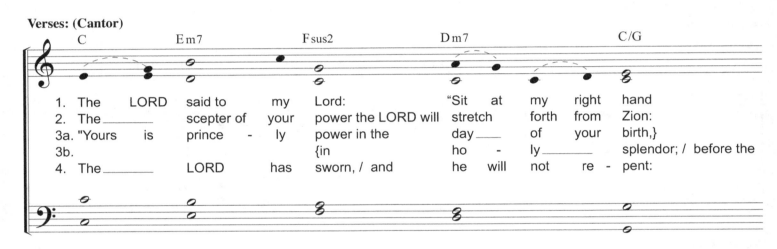

1. The LORD said to my Lord: "Sit at my right hand
2. The _____ scepter of your power the LORD will stretch forth from Zion:
3a. "Yours is prince - ly power in the day ____ of your birth,}
3b. {in ho - ly _____ splendor; / before the
4. The _____ LORD has sworn, / and he will not re - pent:

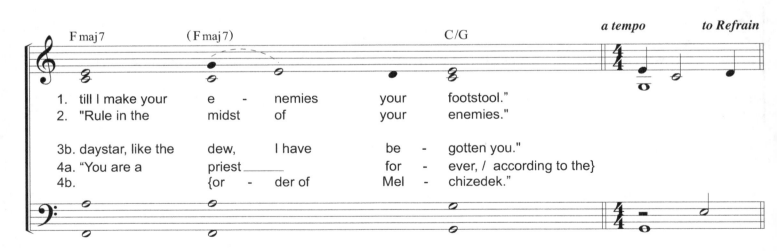

a tempo   *to Refrain*

1. till I make your e - nemies your footstool."
2. "Rule in the midst of your enemies."

3b. daystar, like the dew, I have be - gotten you."
4a. "You are a priest ____ for - ever, / according to the}
4b. {or - der of Mel - chizedek."

Gospel Acclamation: John 6:51

Acclamation: (Keyboard/SATB) NO. II

(M.M. ♩ = c. 130)

Al - le - lu - ia, al - le - lu - ia, al - le - lu - ia._____

Verse: (Cantor)

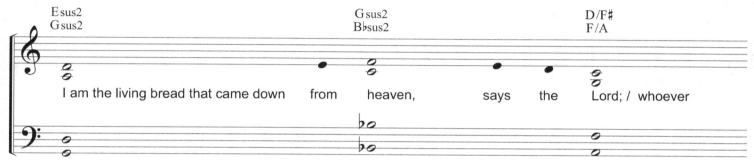

I am the living bread that came down from heaven, says the Lord; / whoever

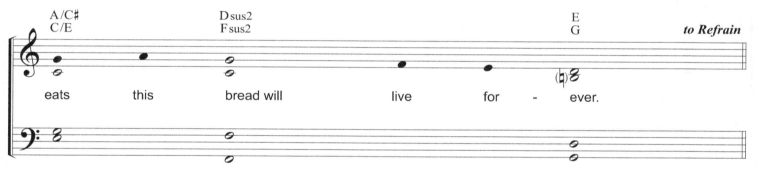

eats this bread will live for - ever.

13th Sunday in Ordinary Time

June 30

Psalm 16:1-2, 5, 7-8, 9-10, 11

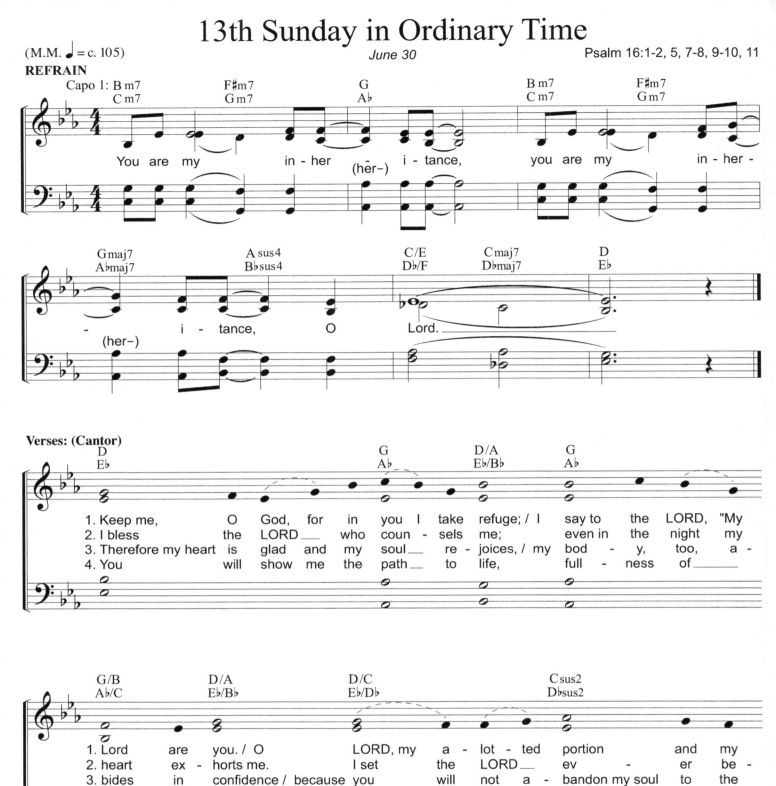

Gospel Acclamation: 1 Samuel 3:9; John 6:68c

Acclamation: (Keyboard/SATB) NO. IV

(M.M. ♩ = c. 116)

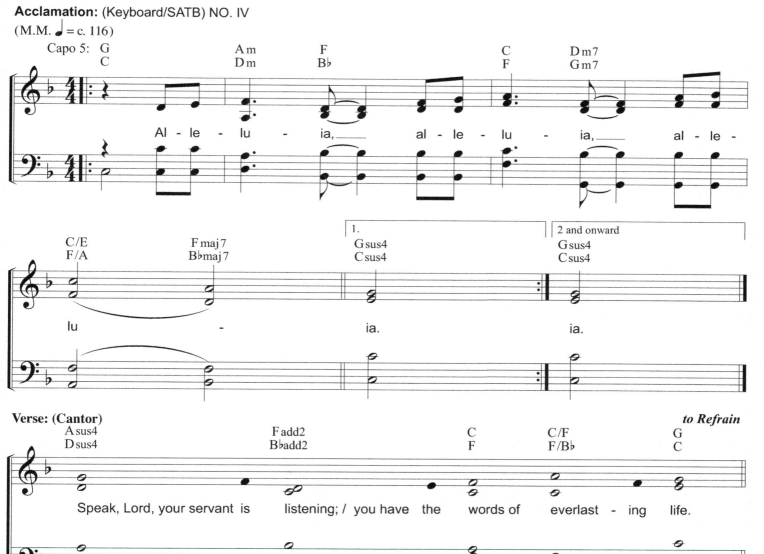

Verse: (Cantor)

Speak, Lord, your servant is listening; / you have the words of everlast - ing life.

14th Sunday in Ordinary Time

July 7

(M.M. ♪ = c. 158)

Psalm 66:1-3, 4-5, 6-7, 16, 20

REFRAIN [or: Alleluia]

Let all the earth cry out, let all the earth cry out, let all the earth cry out to God with joy.

Verses: (Cantor)

1. Shout joy - ful - ly to God, all the earth, / sing praise to the
2. "Let all the earth worship and sing praise to you, / sing praise to
3. He has changed the sea in - to dry land; / through the riv - er they
4. Hear now, all you who fear God, / while I de - clare what

1. glory of his name; pro - claim his glo - rious praise.
2. your name!" / Come and see the works of God, / his tre -
3. passed on foot; / there - fore let us re - joice in him. / He
4. he has done for me. (--) Blessed be God / who re -

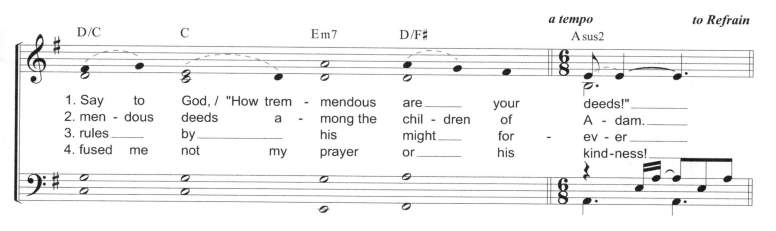

1. Say to God, / "How trem - mendous are _____ your deeds!" _____
2. men - dous deeds a - mong the chil - dren of A - dam. _____
3. rules _____ by _____ his might _____ for - ev - er _____
4. fused me not my prayer or _____ his kind-ness!

Gospel Acclamation: Colossians 3:15a, 16a

Acclamation: (Keyboard/SATB) NO. I

Al - le - lu - ia, al - le - lu - ia, al - le - lu - ia.

Verse: (Cantor)

to Refrain

Let the peace of Christ con-trol your hearts; / let the word of Christ dwell in you richly.

15th Sunday in Ordinary Time

July 14

Psalm 69:14, 17, 30-31, 33-34, 36, 37

For alternate **Responsorial Psalm**, see *Lectionary for the Mass, Second Typical Edition #105.*

Gospel Acclamation: cf. John 6:63c, 68c

Acclamation: (Keyboard/SATB) NO. I

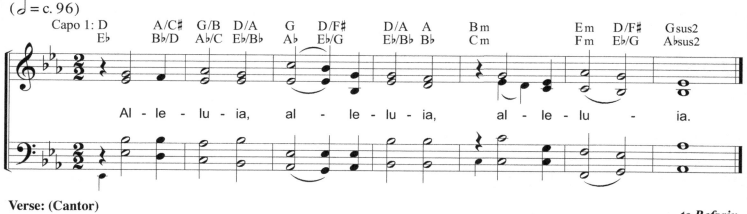

Verse: (Cantor)

16th Sunday in Ordinary Time

July 21

(M.M. ♩ = c. 104)

REFRAIN

Psalm 15:2-3, 3-4, 4-5

He who does jus-tice will live in the pres-ence of the Lord.____

Verses: (Cantor)

1. One who walks blameless - ly and does
2. Who____ harms not his fel - low man, nor takes up a re -
3. Who____ lends not his money at usury and accepts no

1. justice; (------------------) who thinks the truth in his
2. proach against his neighbor; by whom the reprobate is____ de -
3. bribe against the innocent. One who does these things shall never be dis -

a tempo   to Refrain

1. heart and____ slanders not with his tongue.
2. spised, while he honors those who fear the LORD.
3. turbed, [shall____ never be dis - turbed.]

Gospel Acclamation: cf. Luke 8:15

Acclamation: (Keyboard/SATB) NO. II

(M.M. ♩ = c. 130)

Capo 3: A
C

| G | D/F♯ | E | E/D | A/C♯ | D | D/F♯ | Esus4 | E |
| Bb | F/A | G | G/F | C/E | F | F/A | Gsus4 | G |

Al - le - lu - ia, al - le - lu - ia, al - le - lu - ia. _____

Verse: (Cantor)

Esus2   Gsus2   D/F♯
Gsus2   Bbsus2   F/A

Blessed are they who have kept the word with a gen - er - ous heart / and

to Refrain

A/C♯   Dsus2   E
C/E   Fsus2   G

yield   a   harvest through per - se - verance.

17th Sunday in Ordinary Time

July 28

Psalm 138:1-2, 2-3, 6-7, 7-8

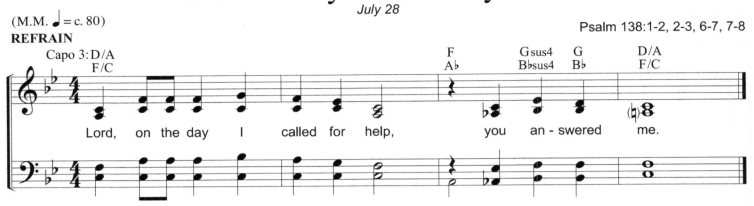

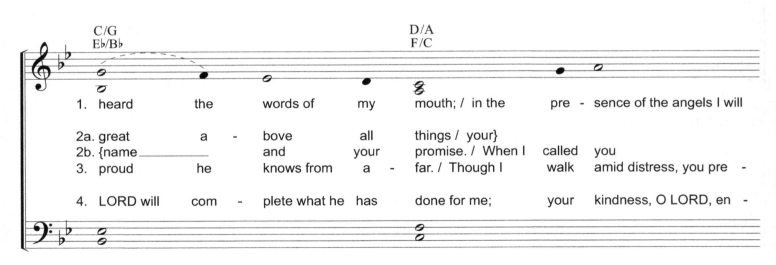

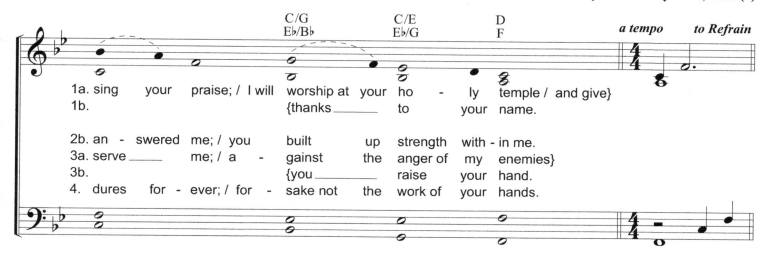

1a. sing your praise; / I will worship at your ho - ly temple / and give}
1b. {thanks_____ to your name.

2b. an - swered me; / you built up strength with - in me.
3a. serve_____ me; / a - gainst the anger of my enemies}
3b. {you_____ raise your hand.
4. dures for - ever; / for - sake not the work of your hands.

Gospel Acclamation: Romans 8:15bc
Acclamation: (Keyboard/SATB) NO. III

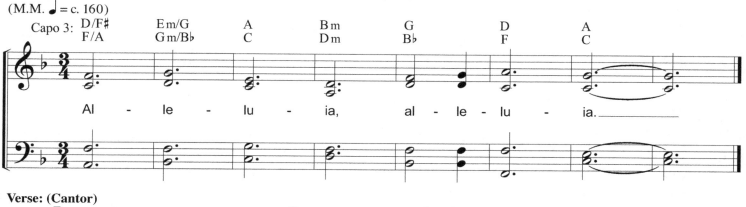

Al - le - lu - ia, al - le - lu - ia._____

Verse: (Cantor)

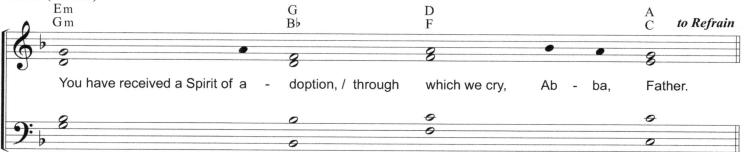

You have received a Spirit of a - doption, / through which we cry, Ab - ba, Father.

18th Sunday in Ordinary Time

August 4

Gospel Acclamation: Matthew 5:3

Acclamation: (Keyboard/SATB) NO. III

Al - le - lu - ia, al - le - lu - ia.

Verse: (Cantor)

Blessed are the poor in spirit, / for theirs is the king - dom of heaven.

to Refrain

19th Sunday in Ordinary Time

August 11

(M.M. ♪ = c. 112)

Psalm 33:1, 12, 18-19, 20-22

REFRAIN

Bless-ed the peop-le the Lord has cho-sen, the Lord has cho-sen to be his own.

Verses: (Cantor)

1. Ex - ult, _____ you just, in the LORD; praise from the up - right is fit - ting. Blessed the nation whose God is the LORD, / the people he has chosen for his own inher - i - tance.

2. See, the eyes of the LORD are up - on those who fear him, / upon those who hope for his kind - ness, / To de - liv - er them from death and pre - serve them in spite of fam - ine.

3. (—) Our _____ soul waits for the LORD, / who is our help and our shield. _____ / May your kindness, O LORD, be up - on us / who have put _____ our hope _____ in _____ you.

a tempo *to Refrain*

Gospel Acclamation: Matthew 24:42a, 44

Acclamation: (Keyboard/SATB) NO. II

(M.M. ♩ = c. 130)

Verse: (Cantor)

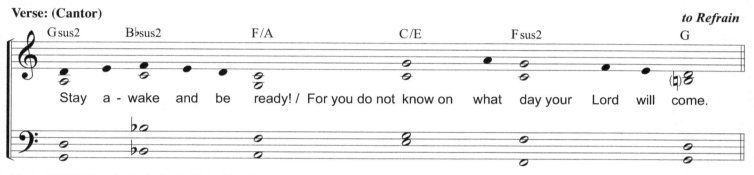

The Assumption of the Blessed Virgin Mary:
At the Vigil Mass

August 14

Gospel Acclamation: Luke 11:28
Acclamation: (Keyboard/SATB) NO. III

The Assumption of the Blessed Virgin Mary:
At the Mass during the Day

August 15

Psalm 45:10, 11, 12, 16

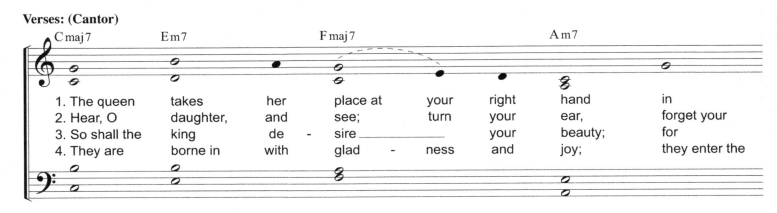

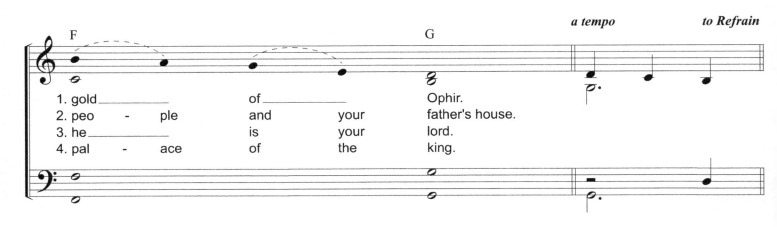

Gospel Acclamation:

Acclamation: (Keyboard/SATB) NO. III

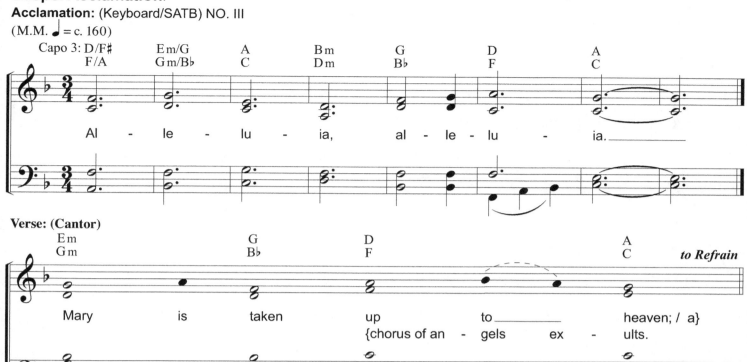

Verse: (Cantor)

20th Sunday in Ordinary Time
August 18

Gospel Acclamation: John 10:27

Acclamation: (Keyboard/SATB) NO. IV

(M.M. ♩ = c. 116)

Al - le - lu - ia, al - le - lu - ia, al - le -

lu - ia. ia.

Verse: (Cantor)

My sheep hear my voice, says the Lord; / I know them, and they follow me.

21st Sunday in Ordinary Time

August 25

Gospel Acclamation: John 14:6

Acclamation: (Keyboard/SATB) NO. I

Verse: (Cantor) *to Refrain*

I am the way, the truth and the life, says the Lord; / no one comes to the Father, ex-cept through me.

Music: *Mass of the Sacred Heart*; Timothy R. Smith © 2007, 2010, Timothy R. Smith. Published by OCP. All rights reserved.

22nd Sunday in Ordinary Time

September 1

Psalm 68:4-5, 6-7, 10-11

www.timothyrsmith.com

Gospel Acclamation: Matthew 11:29ab

Acclamation: (Keyboard/SATB) NO. II

(M.M. ♩ = c. 130)

Al - le - lu - ia, al - le - lu - ia, al - le - lu - ia.

Verse: (Cantor)

to Refrain

Take my yoke up - on you, says the Lord, / and learn from me, / for I am meek and hum - ble of heart.

23rd Sunday in Ordinary Time

September 8

Psalm 90: 3-4, 5-6, 12-13, 14,17

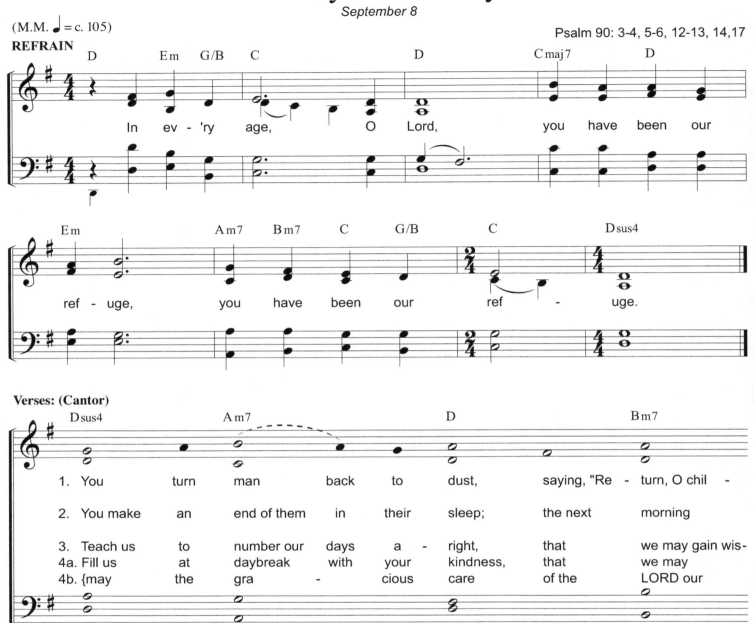

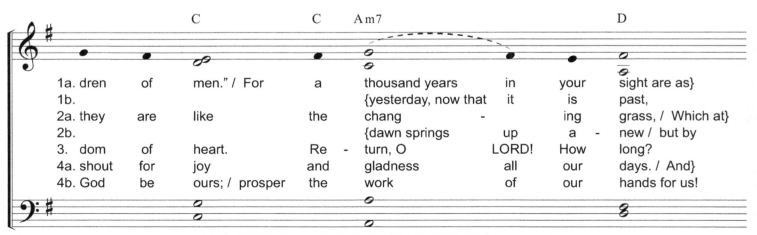

Through composed octavo Ed. 92446 and through composed with SATB
Refrain in *With the Lord* songbook Ed. 10581, both available at www.ocp.org.

144

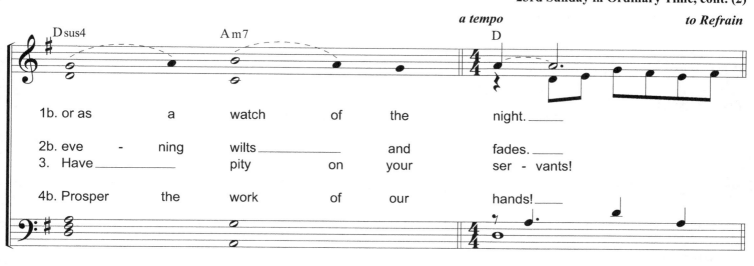

1b. or as a watch of the night.___
2b. eve - ning wilts___ and fades.___
3. Have___ pity on your ser - vants!
4b. Prosper the work of our hands!___

Gospel Acclamation: Psalm 119:135

Acclamation: (Keyboard/SATB) NO. IV

(M.M. ♩ = c. 116)

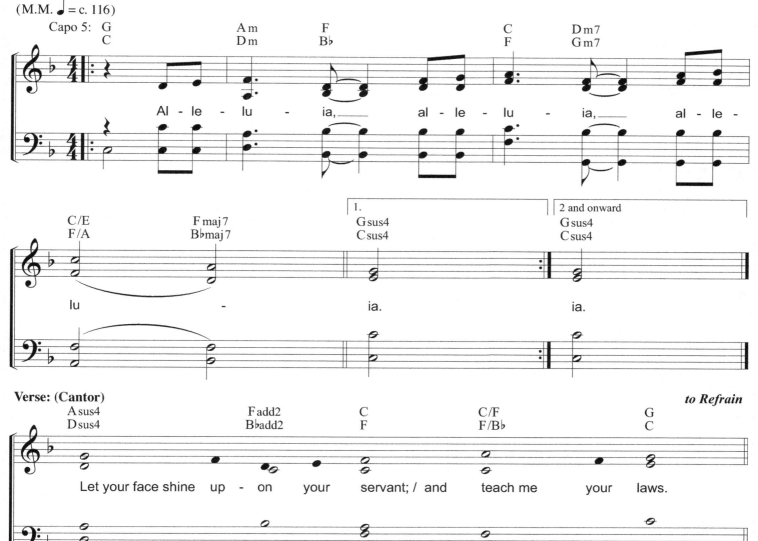

Al - le - lu - ia, al - le - lu - ia,___ al - le -

lu - ia. ia.

Verse: (Cantor) *to Refrain*

Let your face shine up - on your servant; / and teach me your laws.

24th Sunday in Ordinary Time

September 15

Gospel Acclamation: 2 Corinthians 5:19

Acclamation: (Keyboard/SATB) NO. IV

(M.M. ♩ = c. 116)

Verse: (Cantor)

God was re - con - ciling the world to him - self in Christ / and en -}
{trusting to us the message of reconcil - i - ation.

25th Sunday in Ordinary Time

September 22

(M.M. ♩ = c. 88)

REFRAIN [or: Alleluia]

Psalm 113:1-2, 4-6, 7-8

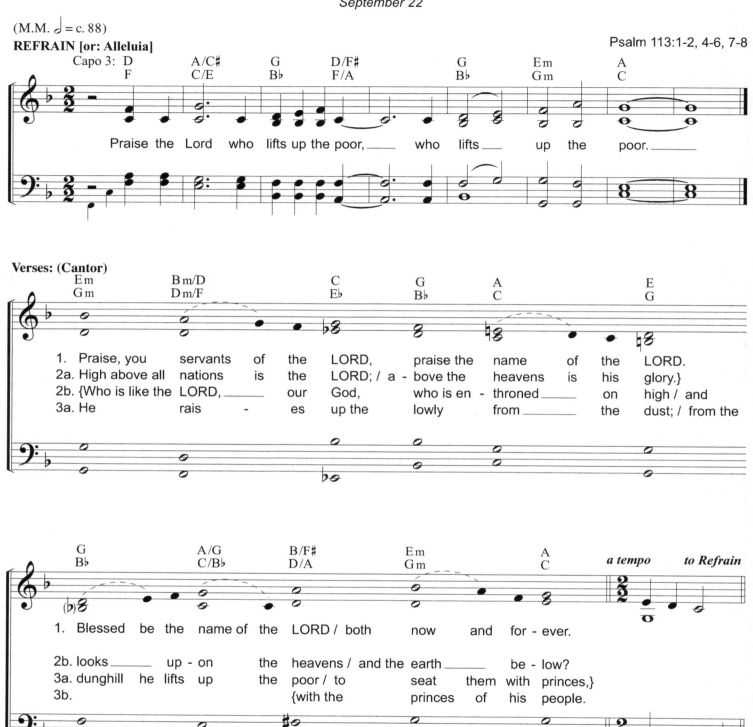

Praise the Lord who lifts up the poor, _____ who lifts _____ up the poor. _____

Verses: (Cantor)

1. Praise, you servants of the LORD, praise the name of the LORD.
2a. High above all nations is the LORD; / a - bove the heavens is his glory.}
2b. {Who is like the LORD, _____ our God, who is en - throned _____ on high / and
3a. He rais - es up the lowly from _____ the dust; / from the

1. Blessed be the name of the LORD / both now and for - ever.

2b. looks _____ up - on the heavens / and the earth _____ be - low?
3a. dunghill he lifts up the poor / to seat them with princes,}
3b. {with the princes of his people.

a tempo   *to Refrain*

Gospel Acclamation: 2 Corinthians 8:9

Acclamation: (Keyboard/SATB) NO. IV

(M.M. ♩ = c. 116)

Capo 5:

Lyrics:
Al - le - lu - ia, ___ al - le - lu - ia, ___ al - le -
lu - ia. ia.

Verse: (Cantor)   *to Refrain*

Though our Lord Je - sus Christ was rich, he be - came poor,}
{so that by his poverty you might be - come rich.

26th Sunday in Ordinary Time

September 29

Gospel Acclamation: 2 Corinthians 8:9

Acclamation: (Keyboard/SATB) NO. IV

(M.M. ♩ = c. 116)

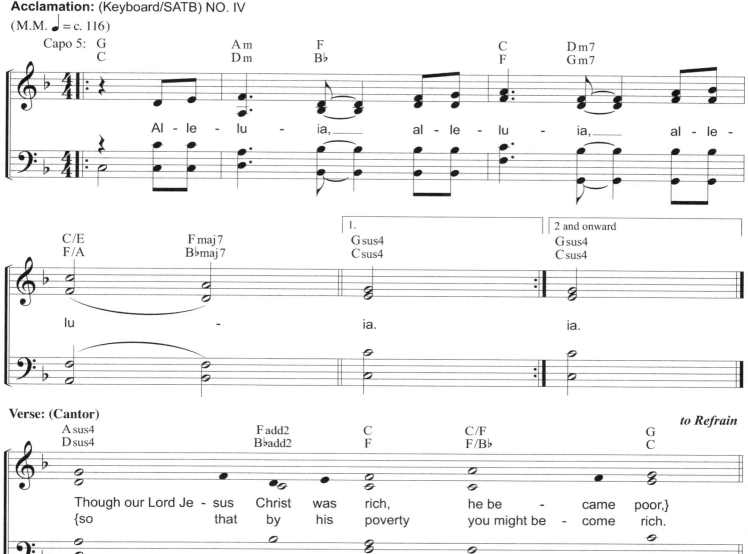

Verse: (Cantor)

to Refrain

Though our Lord Je - sus Christ was rich, he be - came poor,}
{so that by his poverty you might be - come rich.

27th Sunday in Ordinary Time

October 6

Psalm 95:1-2, 6-7, 8-9

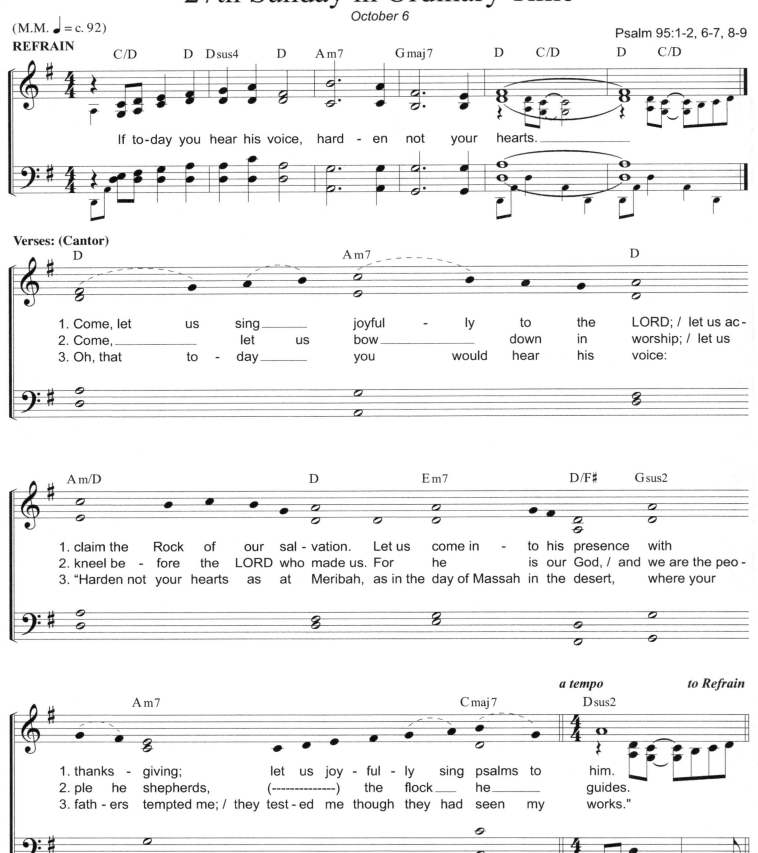

Gospel Acclamation: 1 Peter 1:25

Acclamation: (Keyboard/SATB) NO. I

Verse: (Cantor)

to Refrain

The word of the Lord re - mains for - ever. / This is   the word that has been pro - claimed to you.

28th Sunday in Ordinary Time
October 13

Gospel Acclamation: 1 Thessalonians 5:18

Acclamation: (Keyboard/SATB) NO. II

(M.M. ♩ = c. 130)

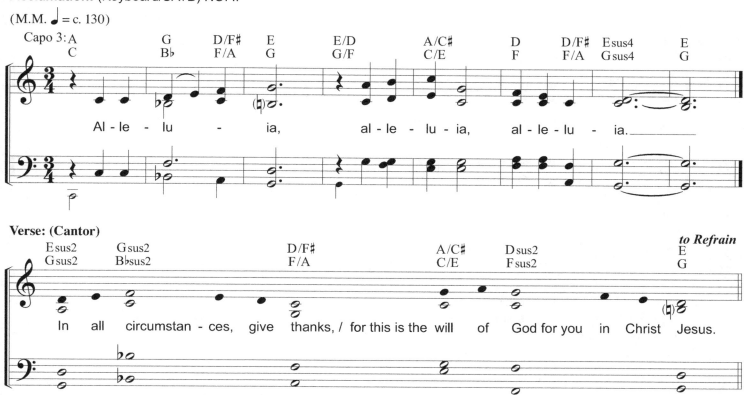

Al - le - lu - ia, al - le - lu - ia, al - le - lu - ia._____

Verse: (Cantor)

to Refrain

In all circumstan - ces, give thanks, / for this is the will of God for you in Christ Jesus.

29th Sunday in Ordinary Time

October 20

(M.M. ♩ = c. 100)

Psalm 121:1-2, 3-4, 5-6, 7-8

REFRAIN Capo 3:

Our help is from the Lord, who made heav-en and earth.

Verses: (Cantor)

1. I lift up my eyes toward the mountains; / whence shall
2. May he not suffer your foot to slip; / may he
3. The LORD is your guard - ian, the LORD is your shade; / he is be-
4. The LORD will guard you from all evil;

1. help come to me? My help is from _____ the
2. slumber not who guards you: in - deed he neither slum - bers nor
3. side you at your right hand. The sun shall not harm you by
4. he will guard your life. The LORD will guard your com - ing and

a tempo *to Refrain*

1. LORD, who made heav - en and earth.
2. sleeps, the _____ guard - ian of Israel.
3. day, nor the moon _____ by night.
4. going, both _____ now and for - ever.

Gospel Acclamation: Hebrews 4:12

Acclamation: (Keyboard/SATB) NO. I

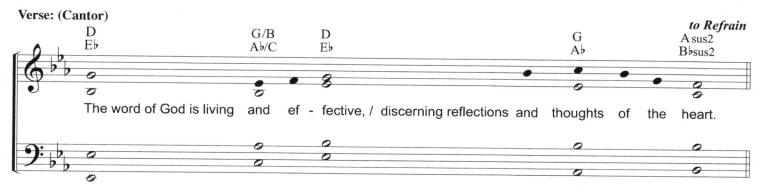

Verse: (Cantor)

The word of God is living and ef‑fective, / discerning reflections and thoughts of the heart.

30th Sunday in Ordinary Time

October 27

Psalm 34:2-3, 17-18, 19, 23

Gospel Acclamation: 2 Corinthians 5:19
Acclamation: (Keyboard/SATB) NO. III

All Saints

November 1

Psalm 24:1bc-2, 3-4ab, 5-6

Verses: (Cantor)

1. The LORD's are the earth and its fullness; / the world and those who dwell in it. / For he founded it up-on the seas and es-tablished it up-on the riv-ers.
2. Who can ascend the mountain of the LORD? / or who may stand in his ho-ly place? One whose hands are sinless, / whose heart is clean, who de-sires not what is vain.
3. He shall receive a blessing from the LORD, / a re-ward from God his sav-ior. Such is the race that seeks him, / that seeks the face of the God of Ja-cob.

Gospel Acclamation: Matthew 11:28

Acclamation: (Keyboard/SATB) NO. I

Al - le - lu - ia, al - le - lu - ia, al - le - lu - ia.

Verse: (Cantor)

to Refrain

Come to me, all you who labor and are burdened, / and I will give you rest, says the Lord.

Music: *Mass of the Sacred Heart*; Timothy R. Smith, © 2007, 2010, Timothy R. Smith. Published by OCP. All rights reserved.

31st Sunday in Ordinary Time

November 3

Psalm 145:1-2, 8-9, 10-11, 13, 14

REFRAIN

I will praise your name for ev - er, my king and my God. *(Keyboard)*

Verses: (Cantor)

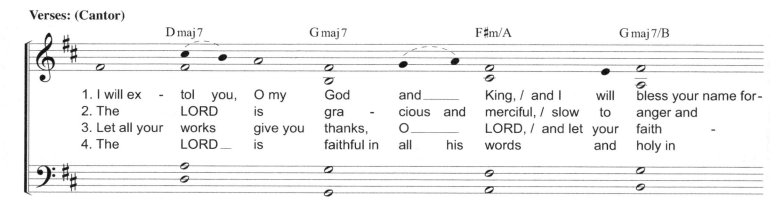

1. I will ex - tol you, O my God and King, / and I will bless your name for-
2. The LORD is gra - cious and merciful, / slow to anger and
3. Let all your works give you thanks, O LORD, / and let your faith -
4. The LORD is faithful in all his words and holy in

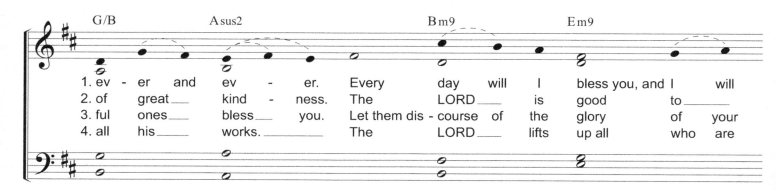

1. ev - er and ev - er. Every day will I bless you, and I will
2. of great kind - ness. The LORD is good to
3. ful ones bless you. Let them dis - course of the glory of your
4. all his works. The LORD lifts up all who are

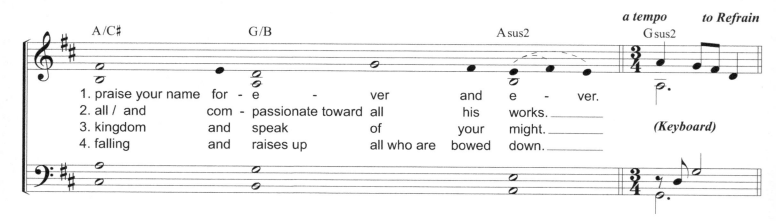

1. praise your name for - e - ver and e - ver.
2. all / and com - passionate toward all his works.
3. kingdom and speak of your might.
4. falling and raises up all who are bowed down.

(Keyboard)

Gospel Acclamation: John 3:16

Acclamation: (Keyboard/SATB) NO. IV

(M.M. ♩ = c. 116)

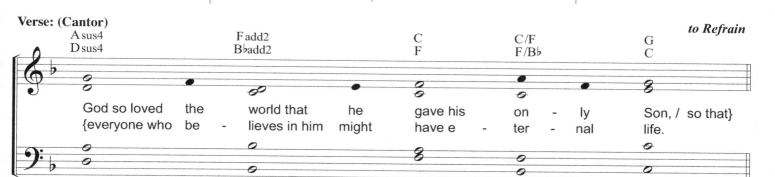

Verse: (Cantor)

to Refrain

God so loved the world that he gave his on - ly Son, / so that}
{everyone who be - lieves in him might have e - ter - nal life.

32nd Sunday in Ordinary Time

November 10

Psalm 17:1, 5-6, 8, 15

www.timothyrsmith.com

Gospel Acclamation: Revelation 1:5a, 6b
Acclamation: (Keyboard/SATB) NO. III
(M.M. ♩ = c. 160)

Al - le - lu - ia, al - le - lu - ia.

Verse: (Cantor)

to Refrain

Je - sus Christ is the firstborn of the dead; / to}
{him be glory and power, / forev - er and ever.

33rd Sunday in Ordinary Time

November 17

Psalm 98:5-6, 7-8, 9

REFRAIN

The Lord comes to rule the earth with jus - tice.

Verses: (Cantor)

1. Sing_____ praise to the LORD with the harp, with the harp and melo - di - ous
2. Let the sea and what fills it re - sound, the_____ world and those who dwell in
3. Before the LORD, for he comes, for he comes to rule the

1. song. With trumpets and the sound of the horn sing joyfully before the
2. it; / let the rivers clap their hands, the moun - tains shout with
3. earth; / he will rule the world with just - ice / and the peo -

a tempo   *to Refrain*

1. King, the LORD._____
2. them for joy.
3. ples with e - qui - ty._____

Gospel Acclamation: Luke 21:28

Acclamation: (Keyboard/SATB) NO. IV

(M.M. ♩ = c. 116)

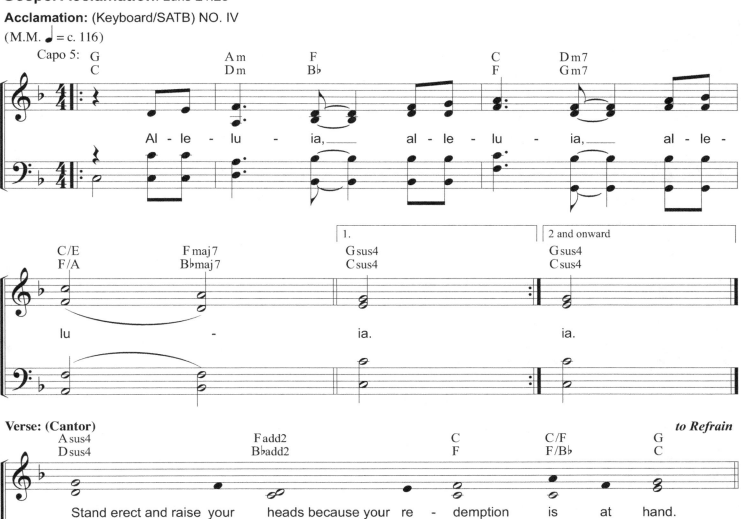

Verse: (Cantor)

to Refrain

Stand erect and raise your heads because your re - demption is at hand.

Music © 2014, Timothy R. Smith. Published by TR TUNE, LLC. All rights reserved.

Our Lord Jesus Christ, King of the Universe

November 24

Gospel Acclamation: Mark 11:9,10

Acclamation: (Keyboard/SATB) NO. V

(M.M. ♪ = c. 150)

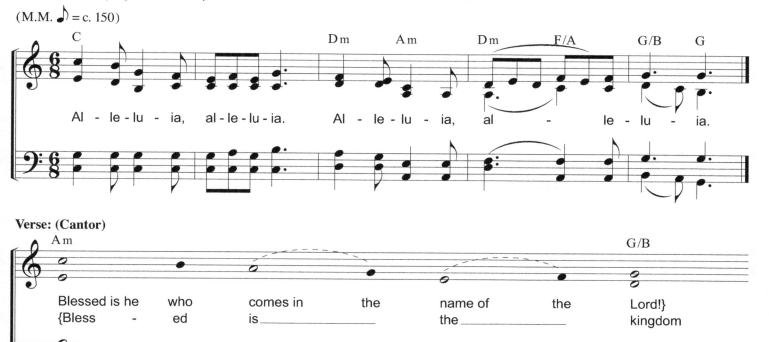

Verse: (Cantor)

Thanksgiving Day

November 28

For alternate **Responsorial Psalms**, see *Lectionary for the Mass, Second Typical Edition* #945.

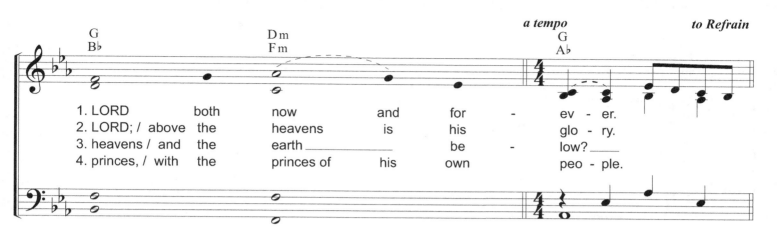

1. LORD both now and for - ev - er.
2. LORD; / above the heavens is his glo - ry.
3. heavens / and the earth be - low?
4. princes, / with the princes of his own peo - ple.

Gospel Acclamation: 1 Thessalonians 5:18 (946.7)

Acclamation: (Keyboard/SATB) NO. II

(M.M. ♩ = c. 130)

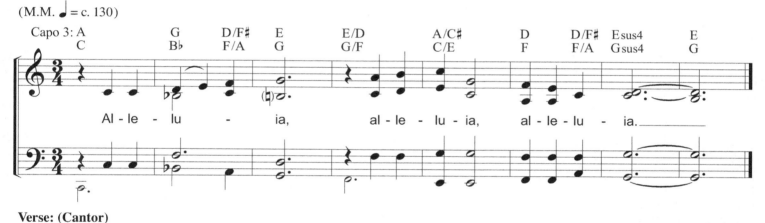

Al - le - lu - ia, al - le - lu - ia, al - le - lu - ia.

Verse: (Cantor)

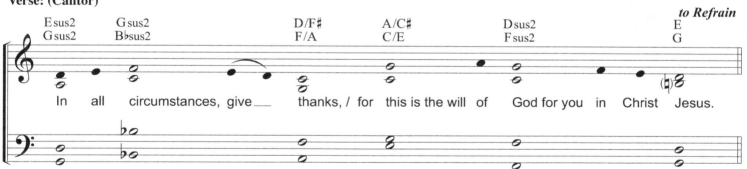

In all circumstances, give thanks, / for this is the will of God for you in Christ Jesus.

For alternate **Gospel Acclamation Verses**, see *Lectionary for the Mass, Second Typical Edition* #946.

Rite of Entrance into the Order of Catechumens

Alternate response: "Lord, let your mercy be on us, as we place our trust in you."

Gospel Acclamation: John 1:41, 17b

Acclamation: (Keyboard/SATB) NO. V

(M.M. ♪ = c. 150)

Al - le -lu - ia, al -le -lu - ia. Al - le -lu - ia, al - le - lu - ia.

We have found the Mes - si - ah: Je - sus Christ, through who came truth__ and__ grace.

to Refrain

Selected Psalm for Weddings

Psalm 128:1-2, 3, 4-5

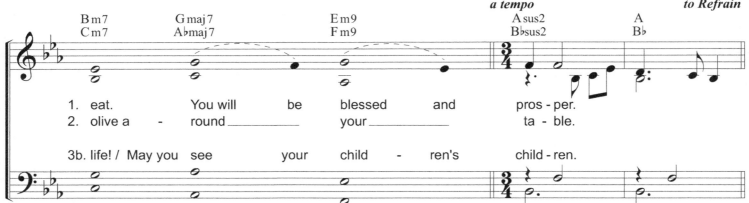

Alternate Response: "See how the Lord blesses those who fear him."

For alternate **Responsorial Psalms** for weddings, see *Lectionary for the Mass, Second Typical Edition* #803.

Selected Psalm for Funerals

Alternate response: "The salvation of the just comes from the Lord."

For alternate **Responsorial Psalms** for funerals, see *Lectionary for the Mass, Second Typical Edition* #1013.

Selected Common (Seasonal) Psalm for Ordinary Time

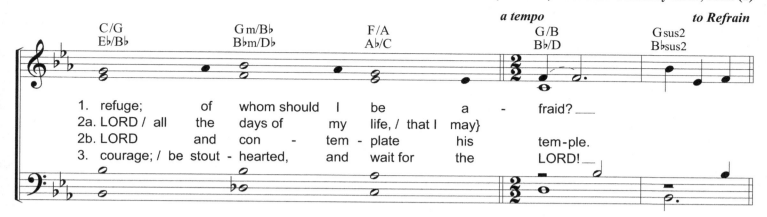

1. refuge;   of   whom should   I   be   a   -   fraid? ___
2a. LORD / all   the   days of   my   life, / that I   may}
2b. LORD   and con - tem - plate   his   tem-ple.
3. courage; / be stout - hearted,   and   wait for   the   LORD! ___

Made in the USA
Middletown, DE
02 December 2018